Scratch That™

SEASONAL MENUS *&* PERFECT PAIRINGS

Scratch That™

SEASONAL MENUS & PERFECT PAIRINGS

CONNIE FAIRBANKS

C & K Press
Chicago, IL   USA

First edition

Published by C&K Publishing, Chicago, Illinois

www.conniefairbanks.com

Edited by Julie Stillman

Cover and interior design by Maritza Medina—M Design

Photographs by Johanna Moya—Diverse Design

Printed in Canada

ISBN 978-0-9790234-0-8

The book is dedicated to my mother and my Aunt Della. Without them, I wouldn't have all the wonderful memories from my childhood. They taught me how to make homemade food from scratch.

Acknowledgments

Special thanks to my husband Kirk Twiss for his love, humor, advice, understanding, and passion for good food and wine. Also, thanks to my editor, Julie Stillman, for her patience and my designer, Maritza Medina, for her creativity.

Thanks to all those who helped with my first cookbook: Kathie Allison, Simone Amorico, Sheila Ainbinder, Greg and Kendell Anderson, Lydia Ballenger, Kristin Beenfeldt, Randi Bergey, Ruth Bok, Maryellen Callanan, Suzanne Ciba, Maggie Crandall, Andrea Culbertson, Jean-Hubert and Marie Yvonne Demeulenaere, Jude and Sal DePaolo, Peter Deveney, Kevin Doney, Donna Filkin, Perry Fotopoulos, Cheryle Gartley, Joan Goldman, Richard Golembeski, Liadain Herriott, Lori Hobscheidt, Susan Imus, Gayla Jones, Mary Lane Kamberg, Carla Kassel, Norma Kuhn, Anne Lavoud, Frank Martin, Michael Mastrocesare, Nancy McCort, Mark McCracken, Linda Meierhoffer, Sharmin McKenny, Ann Marie Nordby, Tina Nilsson, Linda Outlaw, Page Palmer, Julie Paradise, Diane Park, Kah Peng, Ulwyn Pierre, Marcia Ridenour, Dale Robinson, Hubert Schwermer, Jamie Shaak, Mary Grayce Shioleno, June Shulman, Louise Silberman, Betty Scott Smith, Shanna Toms, Patricia True, Alicia Twiss, Alston Twiss, Kristy Wenz, and Twila Williams.

Susie's Birthday Brunch

Champagne with Tangerine Juice
Quince/Parmesan/Arugula Kabobs
Shrimp Salad on Endive
Quail eggs with Chipotle Aïoli
Celery Puree with Pomegranate Molasses

Tomato Basil Soup

Strata with Cheese and Spinach
Asparagus Vinaigrette
Grape, Marcona Almond, and Parsley Salad

Rosé

Pumpkin Apple Cake
Chocolate Mousse

Intelligentsia Coffee
Anise, Pine Nut, and Currant Biscotti

Contents

Introduction

My mother says I have been reading cookbooks, trying some new dishes, or practicing the piano since I was five years old. Somewhere in my very humble beginnings, I read in *Jim Beard's Barbeque Cookbook* to put an ice cube in the middle of a hamburger to keep it moist and juicy. Of course I tried it and it worked, and it still works. Also, during my fast food jobs at Hardee's, I learned that dill pickle juice cleans up the grill quite nicely. That still works too!

Growing up on a farm in Kansas, I didn't realize how fortunate I was to have home-churned butter, fresh cream and milk, and vegetables from our garden to turn those fresh seasonal ingredients into homemade ice cream, wonderful fruit cobblers and vegetable sautés. While homemade snicker doodle cookies were baking, I would be practicing Hanon or learning the piano score for the school play, *Oklahoma*. Every summer, my three sisters and I would prepare for the 4-H County Fair by making our buttermilk biscuits and golden glow cake to win that coveted purple ribbon.

Throughout my corporate career, I continued to entertain friends and family by always experimenting with different recipes and planning menus for six. Obviously, I learned this from my Aunt Della who was doing this in the 1960s for the Family Reunion. What could I prepare, as a home chef, with a busy career and family life? As Julia Child said frequently in her cookbooks, plan, plan, and plan. Do as much as you can do ahead. Plan menus for the week. Then the tasks won't seem so monumental. Also, read recipes several times before you plan to make them to make sure you understand the directions before you start.

Aunt Della's menu planning, circa 1960

I wrote *Scratch That* to give home chefs access to three- and four-course seasonal homemade menus that can be made every day, and with confidence, because the recipes have been tested over and over. However, please treat the recipes as guidelines to your finished outcome. You will tweak the recipes for your own personal tastes.

If you think it is difficult putting together menus, I hope I have taken this worry away from you by providing eighteen menus. The menus are balanced with seasonal ingredients, tastes, ease, textures, variety, color, and calories. In addition to the menus, wine, beer, and other beverage pairings are included to take the guesswork out of wine until you gain more experience in this often intimidating area of meal planning.

Many of the menus can be mixed and matched, or can be pared down to two courses. You may find that some of the menus are good enough for company suppers or special occasions. All menus in *Scratch That* are homemade and accessible to home chefs and their families.

To begin your journey, I start my cookbook with an overview of the requisite kitchen equipment. Many of us don't have the time to make the two-page dessert recipes, but you can use time-saving equipment to your advantage in the kitchen. In my opinion, not all of the new-fangled gadgets are necessary, but some good quality gadgets and equipment save a lot of time in the kitchen. Some absolute necessities are several good knives and a food processor. You have tools at work, at play, and in the car. Why wouldn't you have some basic tools in the kitchen? By using these "tools of the kitchen," you can make homemade fresh food many nights of the week. And don't forget about the old stand-bys that our grandmothers used: an apron, kitchen towels to wipe your hands, and a soap dispenser nearby.

I have also included a "basics" chapter, which you might use over and over again when you need a quick measurements and equivalents chart, need to boil eggs properly for deviled eggs, or you need a homemade chicken stock for that savory soup. I hope you will refer to this chapter often throughout your cooking journey. As an additional time-saver, I have repeated the basic recipes from this chapter when they are part of a recipe, so you don't have to flip back and forth throughout the cookbook, losing your time and patience.

I understand that you don't have sous chefs, but you can recruit whoever is in the kitchen at the time. I realize you can't always find the unusual ingredients that chefs use, but I urge you to visit farmers' markets, or grow your own fruits and vegetables if you can. At a minimum, everyone can grow a small pot of herbs in the kitchen or on the deck. The food will taste so much better if it is fresh, made from scratch, and not out of a bottle, jar, or can. You will also reduce your sodium intake immediately by eating fresh and homemade.

Most of us have not had formal culinary training. We learn on the job in our kitchens every day. Every recipe in this book has my notes to talk you through the recipes, just like your mother, aunt, or a personal instructor would do. I'll tell you where to find all the interesting ingredients or how to make substitutions. All unusual terms are described and spelled phonetically so you will never be intimidated by fancy culinary terms again. Also included are tips to make your meal look as good as it tastes. And as my mother and aunts say, "Don't forget to taste as you go."

There are many ways to broaden your culinary horizons. My Grandpa Fairbanks always hammered the grandkids to eat healthy and from all four food groups! I think he was ahead of his time. If you follow this recommendation, your meal will have visual appeal, nutrition, taste, texture, and variety on a daily basis. Try a new vegetable or fruit every week until you have tried every one in your locale. If you travel abroad, try those local vegetables and fruits too. Make your supper an international experience. Practice new toasts from around the world. I hope you enjoy some of my anecdotal travel stories and exploring the culture of my friends around the world.

Think about taking cooking classes in your area. You might want to give or receive gift certificates for cooking classes. Gain from the experience of the teacher/chef and fellow attendees. Learn what equipment they like, where to buy good-quality ingredients, and where the best farmers' markets are located. Many times you will learn the best tricks from a professional chef who thinks that they are common knowledge. Perhaps you will also make some new friends who are "foodies" too!

I once asked a chef friend why the food at his fine-dining restaurant tasted so good compared to home-cooked food. He said it simply; use the best, the freshest, and the most seasonal ingredients you can find, and your food will taste better overnight.

Experiment—don't be afraid to try new things in the kitchen. If you make a mistake or have a kitchen disaster, it's okay. We've all had cakes leak out the bottom of an old springform pan, or burned garlic in the microwave: it's okay, you will learn from your mistakes every time. I hope you appreciate many of the recipes that have some additional information listed, like don't worry if the dough is curdled, but that doesn't matter, it will turn out fine. Remember, you don't have to be exact with recipes for entrées, sides, soups, and salads, but pastry and desserts do require that you use precise measurements and follow the directions.

Be curious. Keep learning—take classes, talk to chefs, talk to waiters, talk to your wine guy, read cookbooks, subscribe to cooking magazines, take notes on vacations, and go on the Internet. Remember, Julia Child didn't start her culinary training until she was 37.

Have fun in the kitchen. Make preparing meals a family affair. You might be surprised what your husband, children, and friends will enjoy doing in the kitchen. Maybe your kids will want to practice using fractions in recipes. Perhaps your husband likes using your gadgets or making trips to the farmers' market, others might like preparing the coffee, chopping onions, setting the table, or just enjoying the chocolate chip cookie dough. Every meal with friends and family is special and memorable. I still recall a meal about 25 years ago in Milwaukee—I remember eating tempura without the batter because the batter wouldn't adhere to the vegetables. My friends and I were fishing out broccoli and carrots from the bottom of the fondue pot and shivering in our fluorescent ski jackets because the flue didn't work on my apartment fireplace. Create memories for a lifetime, laugh, have fun, eat slowly, enjoy every bite, and make it from scratch.

And if the recipe is more than two pages, go out and have a lovely evening eating pizza and beer, or savoring foie gras and a glass of Sauternes. Cheers!

CHAPTER 1

KITCHEN ESSENTIALS

When I started to stock my kitchen several decades ago, I really didn't know what I needed. I started buying utensils that my mother had in her kitchen. Then I found some additional time-saving gadgets and equipment that would be very useful in the kitchen. Not all of the new-fangled gadgets are necessary for the kitchen, like corn holders, egg separator, electric can opener, etc. However, some of the new tools, like the Microplane, and immersion blender save a lot of time and can be used on a daily basis. Think about how much cooking you are going to do. Are you a baker, a griller, do you just like to make main courses? Then you can decide what equipment you need to stock your kitchen. You might want to refer your friends to the Essentials List on page 10 so they could use it for your bridal, birthday gift, or wish list registries.

Before you purchase expensive equipment like pots and pans, knives, and a food processor, find out if you can observe demonstrations, and actually use the equipment before you purchase it. The Internet has many informational websites for purchasing cooking tools and equipment. Often, department stores will have demonstrations of equipment in their Marketplace sections. Cooking classes are also a good way to ask questions about specific brands of equipment, like knives and food processors. You should buy the equipment that you feel comfortable with and will use often. Also, remember that it will last a long time in your kitchen. Quality equipment is an investment in your kitchen and the meals you

prepare for your family and friends. And by all means don't forget that your hands are great tools in the kitchen!

Must-Have Equipment

Before you add equipment to your kitchen, ask yourself these questions: is it a tool or is it a gadget? Will I use the tool at least once a week? The following is my list of essential kitchen equipment.

Food processor (11 cup): Some uses of the food processor are: making dips, sauces, soups, and spreads; shredding carrots and cabbage; tart crusts, slicing potatoes, shredding hard blocks of Parmesan cheese, and making homemade bread crumbs.

Wooden cutting boards: I recommend a 24x18-inch board for Asian cooking and chopping different types of vegetables, and a mainstream 16x12-inch board for your regular chopping jobs. These boards should never be put in the dishwasher or left in a sink immersed in water. To clean them, use 1 tablespoon of bleach mixed with 6 cups of water. The bleach mixture should be used to clean the board, and to switch from chopping vegetables and fruit to meats and poultry. The boards should be seasoned quarterly with linseed oil purchased at a hardware store. Apply some of the oil to a soft cloth and apply to the cutting board as you would polish furniture. The jury is still out regarding wood versus plastic cutting boards. However, the experts still agree that proper cleaning of the cutting boards with a bleach and water solution is a must.

Measuring utensils: Use *metal* measuring spoon sets and cup sets so the print doesn't rub off in the dishwasher. Also, a 2-cup glass liquid measuring cup is essential for accurate measurement of liquid ingredients like milk, syrups, broths, and water. These measuring utensils can be placed in the dishwasher for easy cleanup. For baking, measuring cups help to ensure consistent results.

Heavy-duty electric mixer: To make pizza dough, cakes, cookies, and to make stiff egg whites, you need a heavy-duty upright mixer. Otherwise, you will inevitably burn up the motor of a hand mixer. Be sure to get a mixer that you can add attachments to, like a pasta maker.

Good-quality pots and pans: You need a 4-quart Dutch oven for stews, polentas, and for braising, 1½ and 3-quart saucepans for boiling eggs, making sauces, simple syrups, puddings, and a 7-quart stockpot for pasta and soups. If you plan to make homemade chicken stock and to steam lobsters, you will need a 12-quart pot. These pots and pans should never go in the dishwasher. Don't buy the "sets" of pots and pans; just buy what you need. Spend money on high-quality pots and pans that you will use routinely. Some things to keep in mind when buying pots and pans are: weight, how they feel in your hand, type of handles, cost, and cleanup.

Skillets: You need a 10-inch skillet for routine cooking of dishes like scrambled eggs, frittatas that can go into the oven, and fresh fish, like salmon. It is also nice to have a 12-inch skillet for preparing French toast for a crowd, paella, and family-sized meals. Don't buy skillets with plastic handles, you want them to go into the oven for some meals. A chef's trick is to begin browning pork chops, salmon fillets, etc., on the stove and finishing them in the oven.

Good-quality knives: All you really need is an 8–14-inch chef's knife (costs around $100, but should last a lifetime) for most chopping jobs, a paring knife, a serrated knife for cutting bread, and sharpening tools. Make sure the chef's knife fits your hand so that it feels very comfortable. If this knife fits, it will become your best friend! Spend your money on individual knives, not sets. When you buy a knife set with a block, most of the quality is in the wooden block, not the knives. Instead, hang the individual knives on a metallic strip on your wall, or use a space-saving tray that holds knives in one of your kitchen drawers. Then your knives are within easy reach. Never put your knives in the dishwasher. To clean them, wash them in sudsy water, and then immerse them in a bleach solution. If you take care of your knives properly, they should last a lifetime. Take a knife skills class at a local cooking school to work with various knives and learn how to care for them properly.

Toaster oven: Get the 14-inch model for toasting small amounts of bread, heating single or small meals, toasting nuts, heating appetizers, etc.

Roasting pan and rack (11x15 inches): This is ideal for roasting pork tenderloins, whole chickens and turkeys, beef tenderloin, etc.

Heavy-duty tongs (13 inch) that are padded and feel good in your hand. You can also use them for grilling, stirring, turning pieces of French toast, turning meat while browning it, stirring pasta and sauces, etc.

Immersion blender and mini food processor (400 watt turbo): This works well to liquefy a soup right in the pot so you don't have to transfer it in batches to a food processor. The immersion blender with a mini food processor and whip attachment is handy for whipping cream and for small food processor jobs of 1 cup.

Good-quality rubber scrapers in several different sizes: 6-, 12- and 13-inch scrapers are useful. Make sure the wood handle is sturdy, and the rubber is flexible. It is important to buy them just in the size you need, not in a pre-packaged assortment.

Inexpensive plastic pepper mill that's easy to refill. I always grind fresh whole peppercorns when a recipe calls for pepper.

Metal colanders (8 inch and 12 inch): These are very helpful for draining pasta and draining and rinsing vegetables. These colanders can go into the dishwasher for easy cleaning. Metal colanders seem to last longer than plastic ones.

Microplane and zester: The Microplane is a very useful gadget for grating fresh nutmeg and fine citrus zest. A zester is useful for long thin shreds of citrus zest. Practice with these gadgets before you purchase them.

Wire whisks: You should have an 8-inch whisk for very small jobs like whisking an egg or a small vinaigrette, and an 11-inch whisk for larger jobs like making sauces, gravies, and puddings on the stove.

Heat-resistant potholders: Keep these handy by the oven, and use for grilling too. The mitts work very well.

Inexpensive juicer: A glass juicer is preferred over plastic because it will last a long time with dishwasher cleaning. Make sure it can hold the juice of several oranges and separates the pulp and seeds from the juice.

Pyrex bowls for pre-prep: Use small 3½-inch and 5-inch bowls for holding chopped vegetables, pre-prep of dry ingredients, and for garnishes.

Salad spinner: If you make fresh garden salads, this is a must. The design of salad spinners keeps improving. Look for a plastic spinner that is convenient for your use, and one that you can grip easily with your hand. After you buy your greens and Italian flat-leaf parsley: clean and spin your greens, let them sit on a paper towel on your counter for an hour or so, and then wrap them in a paper towel, and place in a large ziplock bag. They should keep in the refrigerator for a week and are ready when you need them.

Can opener: Have a good quality one that's comfortable to your hand and is padded.

Heat diffuser: An 8-inch heat diffuser is very important for reducing the heat from flames on a gas stove to very low temperatures. On most gas ranges, you cannot turn the flame low enough for some preparations like making sauces or simmering main dishes. Heat diffusers are available at hardware and specialty food stores for under $20.

Set of mixing bowls, glass or metal: Four different sizes from 6-cup to 2-cup.

Wooden spoons: Use 12-inch spoons for mixing soft doughs, and stirring sauces and soups on the stove. These spoons do not conduct heat like metal spoons, and cleanup is easy in the dishwasher. When they start to look very used, just toss them.

Resealable plastic containers with lids: Get different sizes for pre-prep, marinating fish and meat, and for leftovers.

Oven thermometer: Have you ever baked a cake that didn't cook all the way through? Perhaps your oven is not the temperature it says it is. Only a good-quality oven thermometer will tell you for sure. Better yet, have your appliance service representative calibrate your oven. According to one of the leading appliance manufacturers, most home ovens will fluctuate between minus 25 degrees

to plus 25 degrees, which can make a huge difference when baking. Since heating elements are on the bottom of newer ovens, manufacturers do not recommend using aluminum foil to catch drips. If you are using a convection oven, lower the oven temperature about 25 degrees. Convection ovens use constant circulation of air because of the fan, thus you won't need the temperature as high.

Kitchen timer: Most of you will have a timer on your oven or microwave, but if you don't you might consider purchasing a 30- or 60-minute timer. You will find this very handy as you multitask in the kitchen!

Pizza cutter: Whether you eat a lot of pizza from take-out or make it yourself, a pizza cutter is a must!

Quality plastic wrap, aluminum wrap, waxed paper, and parchment paper: Plastic wrap is very useful for microwaving and cover ups for pre-preparation. Aluminum wrap is very useful for covering meat while it rests before carving. Parchment paper is very useful for lining cookie sheets and for lining baking sheets when roasting vegetables. Use waxed paper as a liner to cool freshly baked cookies on a rack, or when icing a cake so that the extra frosting drips on the waxed paper, not your serving platter.

Paper towels: Good for quick cleanup and to prevent splatters in the microwave.

Washable dish towels: These are essential for quick cleanup in the kitchen, and can be reused. Hang them from the dishwasher and cabinet handles. You could also hang a towel rack across the top of the countertop, just above the cabinets and/or dishwasher so they are very accessible.

Plastic storage bags: You should have different sizes for storage of fresh herbs such as parsley, lettuces, leftovers, and vegetables.

Soap dispenser: Located near the kitchen sink for easy and frequent hand washing during food preparation.

Spray bottle of bleach/water mixture: For cleaning knives and cutting boards.

Chalkboard/chalk: Put this in the cooking area of the kitchen so that the grocery list can be started here. Then you won't be racing to the grocery store for last-minute items!

Container to hold most frequently used utensils: Keep this near the stove to hold your whisks, wooden spoons, tongs, or anything used on a daily basis.

Small containers: To hold small amounts of frequently used items like kosher salt, sugar, and olive oil. For olive oil, use your empty wine bottle, and purchase a stopper and pour spout. This makes a very inexpensive attractive container for olive oil. These items will be handy when you need them for food preparation.

Essentials List for Gifts and for Yourself

11-cup food processor
Wooden cutting board
Metal measuring spoons and cup sets
Heavy-duty upright electric mixer
10-inch skillet that can be used in the oven
Dutch oven
7-quart stockpot for soups and pasta
3-quart saucepan
Chef's knife and paring knife
Heavy-duty tongs
Wooden spoons
Microplane
Immersion blender with mini food processor
8- and 11-inch wire whisks
3½ and 5-inch small glass bowls for prepping
Digital oven thermometer
6-, 12-, and 13-inch rubber scrapers
Inexpensive pepper mill

Nice-to-Have Equipment

These items are useful when you decide you will be doing some baking and making lots of family meals. Put them on your future wish lists for birthdays.

▶ Cookie sheets, muffin and cupcake tins, tart pans with removable bottoms
▶ Soufflé dishes
▶ Cake pans (round and oblong), loaf pans
▶ Slow cooker: if you do one-pot meals ahead of time, be sure and purchase one with a removable liner
▶ Grill pan for indoor grilling
▶ Pyrex baking dishes/lids for cobblers and casseroles
▶ Mortar and pestle, wooden and ceramic for grinding herbs
▶ Pastry brush
▶ Potato peeler for peeling vegetables and shaving chocolate or cheese into slices
▶ Potato masher: metal, not plastic
▶ Pancake flipper: metal, not plastic
▶ Ladle: metal, not plastic
▶ Mandoline: for those thinly sliced potatoes and vegetable garnishes that you can't do with a knife or food processor
▶ Funnels for filling olive oil bottles so you don't spill oil on the counter and lose the liquid gold
▶ Garlic press
▶ Garlic holder: ceramic holder with holes if you use lots of garlic for cooking
▶ Digital meat thermometer that can be used for grilling and roasting meats/ poultry
▶ Iced tea pot to make brewed iced tea all year long

BASIC RECIPES AND OTHER KITCHEN KNOW-HOW

I hope this chapter will help you save time in the kitchen. Instead of looking through some 30 cookbooks to find those basic recipes that you never can remember, these "basics" are all here in one place. As a bonus, there are suggestions on how to stock your spice racks and salt bins, how to make the perfect cup of coffee every day, and how to load the dishwasher.

CONNIE'S NOTES: *For different **oils,** try: walnut, hazelnut, or grapeseed oils for a more delicate taste.*

*For different **acids,** try: orange juice, lemon juice, pomegranate juice, lime juice, etc.*

*Additional **herbs** to use are: flat-leaf parsley, thyme, mint, tarragon, dill, chives, etc.*

Emulsifiers: *mustard, hot water, honey, marmalade*

Basic Recipes

The recipes in this section are core recipes that you will use often on your culinary journey.

Vinaigrettes

Generally, the ratio of acid to oil is 1:4 in vinaigrettes, but this is determined by your taste. Eventually, you will be able to eyeball this recipe, and make these vinaigrettes very easily.

1 clove garlic, minced

2 tablespoons red wine vinegar

1 teaspoon fresh lemon juice

1/2 teaspoon kosher salt

1/4 teaspoon freshly ground black pepper

2 teaspoons Dijon mustard

1 tablespoon chopped fresh herbs,
 such as thyme and parsley

1/2 cup extra-virgin olive oil

▶ In a small bowl, combine the garlic, vinegar, lemon juice, salt, pepper, mustard, and herbs. Whisk together, and slowly add the olive oil until it emulsifies. Lightly dress whatever washed and dried greens you prefer for your salad.

Basic Piecrust
for 8- or 9-inch (1 crust) Pie

To make a great piecrust takes lots of practice. Our mothers, aunts, and grandmothers used to make pies every week. Of course they were good at it. They knew just how the dough felt to the hands, when to stop adding flour, and how to roll it out so it wouldn't fall apart. Remember, practice makes perfect. Your friends and family will appreciate a homemade pie!

1 cup flour

1/2 teaspoon kosher salt

1/3 cup plus 1 tablespoon vegetable shortening

2–3 tablespoons ice water

▶ In the bowl of a large food processor, pulse the flour and salt for a few seconds. Add the shortening and process for about 15 seconds until it resembles coarse crumbs. Add the ice water 1 tablespoon at a time, pulse, and keep adding the water until the dough comes together. Remove the dough from the processor bowl, and form into a disk about 6 inches in diameter. Wrap in plastic wrap and refrigerate for at least an hour or overnight.

▶ With a lightly floured rolling pin and board, roll out the dough in a circle about 2 inches larger than your pie pan. Place the dough in the pan, and flute the edges with the overhanging dough. Follow the directions in your own pie recipe from this point.

Basic Piecrust
for 8- or 9-inch (2 crust) Pie

2 cups flour

1 teaspoon kosher salt

$2/3$ cup plus 2 tablespoons vegetable shortening

4–5 tablespoons ice water

▶ Prepare the crust as directed in the one-crust recipe on page 14.

Meringue for Pie

This is the wow factor of a pie from a visual standpoint. Remember the volume of the meringue may be much lower on a high-humidity day.

8-INCH PIE

2 egg whites

$1/4$ teaspoon cream of tartar

$1/4$ cup sugar

$1/4$ teaspoon pure vanilla extract

9–INCH PIE

3 egg whites

$1/4$ teaspoon cream of tartar

6 tablespoons sugar

$1/2$ teaspoon pure vanilla extract

▶ Preheat the oven to 400°F.

▶ Bring the eggs to room temperature by setting them out first thing in the morning. Beat the egg whites and cream of tartar in a very clean glass or metal bowl (free of oil or residue) until foamy. Beat in the sugar 1 tablespoon at a time. Continue beating until stiff and glossy about 4–5 minutes. Beat in the vanilla.

▶ Heap the meringue onto hot pie filling and crust and spread it over the filling. Use a rubber spatula to carefully seal the meringue to the edge of the piecrust to prevent weeping or shrinking. Bake for about 10 minutes or until a delicate brown. Cool away from draft.

CONNIE'S NOTES: *Make sure your bowls and beaters are squeaky clean. Otherwise you will not get stiff peaks.*

Chicken Stock

Homemade chicken stock is an invaluable asset in the kitchen. You will taste the full-bodied flavor difference of homemade chicken stock in soups, vegetables, and chicken pot pie. I like to make a big batch and freeze what I don't use for future use.

Two 4-pound roasting chickens or 8 pounds chicken backs

2 unpeeled parsnips, cut in half

2 large yellow onions with skins on, cut into quarters

2 unpeeled carrots, cut in half

2 stalks celery with leaves, cut in thirds

10 sprigs dill

10 sprigs thyme

10 sprigs flat-leaf parsley

1 head garlic with white paper left on, cut in half lengthwise

8 peppercorns

$1^1/2$ tablespoons kosher salt

▶ Rinse the chickens and discard the giblets. Place the chickens and the rest of ingredients in a large stockpot. Add 5 quarts of water, or just cover the chickens with water. Bring to a boil, uncovered. Reduce the temperature to low, and simmer (uncovered) for about 4 hours.

▶ Strain the entire contents in a very large bowl to catch all of the stock. Discard everything but the cooked chicken. Separate the meat from the bones, skin, and gristle.

(continued)

Save the cooked chicken for a chicken pot pie, chicken salad, or soup. Place the strained stock in the refrigerator or outside in the cold, and let it sit overnight.

▶ Skim off the fat layer from the top of the stock and discard it. Use the stock immediately or freeze it in 2-cup plastic containers.

MAKES ABOUT 4 QUARTS

CONNIE'S NOTES: *Oftentimes you can find inexpensive chicken backs at your grocery store. If not, ask the meat manager if they have chicken backs or ask him to order some for you. After you strain the liquid from the chicken mixture, simply throw away the chicken backs as there is very little meat for reuse.*

Poaching Chicken

Poaching is a very good way to prepare chicken and fish because it adds flavor and helps to retain tenderness. This method of poaching should ensure a juicy chicken breast, not a dried-out one. Poached chicken can be used for chicken salads and sandwiches.

1 carrot

1 stalk celery

1 small onion, roughly chopped

2 whole chicken breasts (with bone in and skin on)

1 fresh bay leaf

1 lemon, sliced

1 teaspoon kosher salt

3 peppercorns

$1/2$ cup white wine

▶ Place the carrot, celery, and onion in the bottom of a medium-sized saucepan and put the chicken breasts on top of the vegetables. Add the bay leaf, lemon, salt, peppercorns, and wine. Just cover the ingredients with chicken stock or water, and turn the heat to high. (The chicken and vegetables should fit tightly in the saucepan.) Bring the liquid to a boil and skim off the foam that forms on top.

▶ Reduce the temperature to low and partially cover the pan. Let the mixture simmer gently until the chicken is finished cooking, about 60 minutes. Check for doneness by piercing the thickest part of the chicken breast, making sure the juices run clear.

▶ Remove the chicken from the pot and let it cool before you cut it, otherwise it will continue cooking in the hot poaching liquid. Discard the bones and skin from the chicken. If you aren't planning to use the chicken for a day or so, return it to the cooled broth and refrigerate. Strain the poaching liquid and use it in soups and for steaming vegetables.

Poaching Fish

This method works well for salmon to be used in a salmon salad.

4–6 cups water

1 medium onion, sliced

3 slices lemon

3 sprigs parsley

1 fresh bay leaf

1 tablespoon kosher salt

2 peppercorns

1 pound fish fillets, with skin on

▶ In a medium-sized skillet, combine the water, onion, lemon, parsley, bay leaf, salt, and peppercorns and bring to a boil. Place the fish in a single layer on top of the boiling poaching liquid. Cover, and simmer 4–6 minutes until the fish flakes easily. Remove the fish from the poaching liquid immediately. Don't overcook the fish.

Fresh Shrimp Preparation

▶ **To cook shrimp:** Partially fill a medium saucepan with water, a bay leaf, 1 tablespoon kosher salt, 4 peppercorns, and a lemon cut in half. Bring to a boil. Add the amount of shrimp that will fit in your pan, and cook until just pink—about 2 minutes. Remove from the stove, and transfer to an ice bath to stop the cooking process.

▶ **To devein shrimp:** Remove the shells of the cooked shrimp just to the tail and discard. On many shrimp, you will see a thin line that is the intestine. Remove this intestine and discard; it should come out in one piece. The shrimp are now ready to eat.

▶ **To grill shrimp:** Devein and remove the partial shells of the shrimp before grilling for a few minutes.

Hard-Boiled Eggs

▶ Carefully place eggs in a medium saucepan. Cover with cold water and add some salt. Bring the water to a boil quickly, uncovered. Then tightly cover the pan; remove from the stove, and let the eggs finish cooking for approximately 22 minutes.

▶ Immediately place the eggs in an ice-water bath to stop the cooking process. When the eggs are cool, peel them and separate the yolks from the whites. The yolks should be a bright lemon color, not a greenish cast, which can happen if they are overcooked. If you are not using the eggs immediately, store in a covered container in the refrigerator for a few days.

White Sauce or Béchamel Sauce

This sauce can be used for scalloped potatoes, macaroni and cheese, lasagna, or any other dish calling for a basic white sauce.

2 cups 2% (low fat) milk

$^1/_2$ stick (4 tablespoons) unsalted butter

$^1/_4$ cup flour

$^1/_2$ teaspoon salt

$^1/_4$ teaspoon pepper

Pinch of freshly grated nutmeg

▶ In a medium saucepan, melt the butter over low heat. Add the flour, stir, and cook until thickened, or 2 minutes. Add the milk and cook over medium heat until thickened and smooth. Set the sauce off the stove. Add whatever ingredients you like, such as cheese or fresh herbs.

MAKES ABOUT 2 CUPS

Béchamel *(bay-shah-MEHL)* is one of the four "mother sauces." It is a milk-based white sauce and is named after its inventor, Louis de Béchamel. The other three mother sauces are: **espagnole** *(ehs-pahn-YOHL)*, a brown stock-based sauce; velouté *(veh-loo-TAY)* a white stock-based sauce; and **allemande** *(ah-leh-MAHND)* an egg-enriched velouté.

Equivalent Measurements

3 teaspoons....1 tablespoon

4 tablespoons....$1/4$ cup

$5^1/3$ tablespoons....$1/3$ cup

8 ounces liquid....1 cup

16 tablespoons....1 cup

2 cups....1 pint

4 cups....1 quart

2 pints....1 quart

4 quarts (liquid)....1 gallon

*If a recipe is written in grams or ounces,
use the Internet/Google to make the
conversion for you. You could also purchase
an inexpensive scale that weighs in grams,
just like chefs use on a day-to-day basis.*

POULTRY COOKING TIMES

Timetable for Roasting a Turkey

Roast turkey (unstuffed) in a 325°F oven
to a minimum internal temperature
of 165°F as follows:

WEIGHT	TIME
4–8 pounds (breast)	$1^1/2$–$3^1/4$ hours
8–12 pounds	$2^3/4$–3 hours
12–14 pounds	3–$3^3/4$ hours
14–18 pounds	$3^3/4$–$4^1/4$ hours
18–20 pounds	$4^1/4$–$4^1/2$ hours
20–24 pounds	$4^1/2$–5 hours

Timetable for Roasting a Chicken

Roast chicken (unstuffed) in a 375–400°F oven
to a minimum internal temperature
of 165°F as follows:

WEIGHT	TIME
3–4 pounds	$1^1/4$–$1^1/2$ hours
5–7 pounds	2–$2^1/4$ hours

Source: USDA Guidelines, 2006

Kirk's Coffee

My husband Kirk makes the best coffee outside of Italy! His actuarial background comes in quite handy when making a cup of smooth, flavorful, and rich-tasting coffee. He believes, like Italian baristas, that good water is the essential ingredient to great-tasting coffee. You may not have the best coffee grinder or coffeepot, but everyone has access to filtered water, either from your refrigerator, a filter on your tap water, or from bottled water.

He measures the water precisely and pours it into the appropriate coffee maker: press pot, drip, or espresso. He takes the fresh beans out of vacuum-tight containers, and grinds the beans to the appropriate grind for the coffeepot. If your favorite coffee is espresso, you might want to invest in a burr grinder that can grind the coffee beans from coarse to fine. The grind of coffee is very important for espresso, because espresso machines force water over finely ground coffee with pressure. Otherwise, an inexpensive grinder will work just fine for drip coffee. You can also grind your beans at the grocery store or coffee store to ensure freshness. Just use the ground coffee within several days so that it is fresh. Very fresh beans are especially helpful when making espresso. If you have a favorite restaurant that makes coffee, ask them what brand they use. In Chicago, many restaurants use Intelligentsia coffee, which is available to the general public.

Decide what your ratio is between ground coffee and water for the desired strength of your brew. Experiment with the measurements and record them until you get them just right. Then you will have the right proportions for that perfect cup of coffee every day. How do you like your coffee to taste: dark and sweet, bitter and creamy, burnt? My husband makes fairly strong coffee by using one coffee scoop (or about two tablespoons of coffee) to six ounces of water.

Keep all of your coffee apparatus together in one place: grinder, coffee maker(s), filters, liquid measuring cup with a lip, measurement tools, coffee scoopers, and tampers. My husband uses tiny brushes to keep the grinder free of residue. Make sure your coffeepot is very clean and also free of residue. Sometimes, a mixture of vinegar and water helps to keep the glass coffeepot meticulously clean.

While any coffeepot will work to brew coffee, glass containers that sit on the heat will eventually burn the coffee. Decide what's most important to you: having your coffee ready when you wake up, dish-washer safe, or storing the brewed coffee in a thermal type container. There are many good coffee websites on the Internet that discuss all the utensils you will need to make the perfect cup of coffee. My husband enjoys www.wholelattelove.com.

By all means enjoy this little bit of heaven every day!

On Spices

Do you ever look in your spice drawer and see spices you haven't used since your last move? Did you move in the last six months? If not, toss those spices. Many of them have lost their potency and will add little to your dishes. As a rule of thumb: whole spices last about a year, and ground spices keep their potency for about six months. Check to see if you can still smell the spices. Also, see if the spices still have vibrant color. If not, toss them! Spices should be kept in sealed containers at room temperature, and away from direct sunlight.

When you decide what types of cuisine you are making, decide which spices you will need to stock. When you are making those Thai or Indian dishes, buy just the amount of spices you need. Spice stores are opening everywhere and they will often sell you small quantities of spices for that special ethnic dish. If possible, buy whole spices and grind them as you need them, just like coffee beans. Plan your spice shopping accordingly, especially during the holidays.

Basic Spices for Your Pantry

Peppercorns (black and white): Buy large quantities and grind them as you need freshly ground pepper

Cayenne red pepper

Cinnamon (ground and cinnamon sticks): If you don't use it all year round, just buy it for the holidays

Red pepper flakes

Whole nutmeg: Grate fresh with a Microplane

Chili powder: Or you can grind whole chilies as you go

Cumin

Spanish paprika: Great smoky flavor for vegetables, eggs, and paellas

Salts

When I was growing up, there was one kind of salt—table salt. Today's cooks have many more options.

Iodized or table salt is the most common form of salt with iodine added. It can have a bitter aftertaste. Iodized salt was manufactured in the 1920s in the Midwest to prevent goiter. Iodine can also be obtained from milk, cheese, and seafood.

Kosher salt is less salty than regular salt, and is free from additives and iodine. Kosher salt contains fewer additives than table salt, and the flakes dissolve easily. You can find kosher salt at grocery stores in three-pound boxes.

Sea salt is considered superior to all kinds of salt and is expensive for everyday use. It is made from seawater using an evaporation process. Save sea salt for finishing dishes. Sea salt can be purchased at specialty stores, or buy it on your vacations to Europe!

Grey salt is from the coast of Brittany, France. It is from the sea so it is natural, moist, and unrefined. It is collected by hand, using Celtic methods. Grey salt is a favorite of chefs.

Fleur de sel is the premier sea salt of Brittany. It is very expensive and sometimes used by chefs to finish entrées.

How to Evaluate a Recipe

Here are some questions to keep in mind when you find recipes online, in a magazine, from a newspaper, from TV, or from a friend.

▶ Read it over. Is it clear? Are there any glaring missing ingredients? More often than not, recipes are not tested.

▶ What's the skill level required to make this recipe?

▶ How much time will it take?

▶ Is the recipe within your budget?

▶ Do you have the proper equipment?

▶ Does it require unusual ingredients? Can you find them? Will you use any leftover ingredients again?

▶ Do you like it? Will your family or friends like it?

▶ Can you change the quantity without altering the recipe?

▶ Does the author have a track record for good recipes?

▶ Will practice make perfect?

What to Wear in the Kitchen and Stay Safe

Comfort and safety are very important for both professional chefs and home chefs. Professional chefs most often cover their arms and legs to protect themselves against burns, scrapes, and hot water. They wear chefs' coats and long pants for a reason. You may want to wear something with long straight sleeves to protect your arms from getting caught in flames on a stove. Chefs worry about falling in the kitchen. Usually, they wear clogs or some type of shoes so they won't slide on grease or water spills on the floor. You might want to consider buying a pair of skid-proof shoes, such as clogs, for your home kitchen too. Chefs often have rubber mats in the kitchen to cushion their feet for long hours of standing in a upright position. These mats can be found at household stores at very reasonable prices for the home chef. You can easily clean these mats in the shower, or outside with a hose and spray nozzle.

Preventing fires is very important to chefs. Keep a fire extinguisher handy for unplanned flareups. Also, keep a box of baking soda handy for small fires in the home kitchen.

Cuts shouldn't be common in the kitchen. Keep your knives sharpened. A dull knife is much more dangerous than a sharp knife. If you don't sharpen your own knives, many cooking stores will professionally sharpen them for a nominal fee. (My husband enjoys doing this task for me. Maybe yours will too.)

Comfort is important to home chefs too. Make sure to wear cotton fabrics that breathe. Cotton fabrics wash very well after repeated washings.

Cleanliness is of the utmost importance in a professional kitchen, and it should be in your kitchen too. Keep a soap dispenser near the kitchen sink for quick hand washings. Then it's near the hot water too. Also, keep a bottle of bleach available for cleaning cutting boards and knives. Just put several tablespoons of bleach in a sink of hot soapy water, and that bleach/water solution should do the trick.

Rubber kitchen mat

How to Load the Dishwasher

After six years of marriage, I have found that my husband is much better at certain tasks in the kitchen than I am. One of those chores is loading the dishwasher so all the dishes get clean and the wineglasses don't get broken. It does take him more time than I would spend loading the dishwasher, but dishes come out sparkling clean the first time around. While you don't have to get out a measuring tape to see if you can load one more plate into your dishwasher, here are some of my husband's tips on loading the dishwasher.

Bad

Good

- Start by rinsing all of the plates and silverware by using a brush to "prewash" the dishes. Remove all egg and pasta mixtures from plates quickly so they don't dry and stick. Then organize all the dishes on the appropriate rack:

  Top rack: glasses, cups, small plastic lids, bowls, and anything horizontal.

  Bottom rack: plates and soup bowls (think vertical), small plates on front rack, and large plates on the back rack.

  Silverware: Put some of the silverware facing up and some facing down—supposedly this ensures even distribution of water flow.

- Remove the silverware basket if you have no silverware or you can save it for another load. You will save lots of valuable space for large serving platters and bowls.

- Find out the type of dishwasher soap that is best for your dishwasher—crystals or liquid—your instructions will specify one or the other. It does make a difference.

- Notice if your shelves are adjustable for those large serving plates, stockpots, or baking dishes.

- Open the door of the dishwasher when the cycle is completed, shake the dishes on the top rack if any water has accumulated, and let the dishes air-dry.

- If you have expensive wineglasses, such as Riedel glasses, invest in wine racks for the dishwasher. The special wine racks for the dishwasher will ensure that the glasses will not break, and dry spotless.

- **Don't** put a large stockpot (face side down) in the bottom shelf of the dishwasher—very little water will reach the top shelf if there are dirty dishes there.

- **Don't** put dishes on top of each other—there needs to be space between them so the water can clean the dishes properly.

SPRING & SUMMER
MENUS

This is an Italian-inspired brunch alive with fresh fruit and vegetables, and heralding spring. I think a couple of the challenges of brunch are not to become a short-order cook and not to turn the meal into cholesterol overload. The highlight of the menu is a lovely strata, which is an updated version of the perennial breakfast casserole. This one adds spinach and subtracts sausage to keep the calories down. The strata oozes creamy cheese, fluffy eggs, and bread, and is topped with Parmesan cheese for crunch.

You can pass the appetizers and mimosas, and serve the rest of the meal buffet style. Be sure to use freshly squeezed orange juice with the Prosecco. Your family and guests will notice the difference. Wrap a melon chunk with a long piece of fresh chive tied into a bow, and place on a decorative plate with slices of prosciutto. Drizzle the melon and prosciutto with extra-virgin olive oil and freshly ground black pepper. Have wedges of lime nearby for bursts of flavor. If black or green figs are in season, slice them into halves or wedges and pile them in the center of the platter. Your family will love the new presentation of prosciutto, figs, and melon.

Take that beautiful crystal punch bowl out of its original wrappings, and use it to serve the pomegranate and pineapple punch on the buffet table. Then your family can take what they want, and it is more brunch casual. However, that doesn't mean your dining table has to be plain. Pull out your pastel placemats and napkins, and dress the table for spring. Buy bunches of pink tulips and beautiful yellow daffodils, and place them in a beautiful vase. Spring has sprung! *Cin Cin!*

The Day Before

▶ **Make the shrimp salad**
▶ **Make the fava spread**
▶ **Peel, seed, and slice the melon**
▶ **Blanch the asparagus**
▶ **Chill the juices and Prosecco**
▶ **Prepare the strata to baking stage**

Weekend Brunch

Parmesan and Quince Skewers

Shrimp Salad on Endive Spears

Fava Bean Spread on
Mini Toasts

Prosecco with Freshly Squeezed
Blood-Orange Juice

Pomegranate and Pineapple Punch

Breakfast Strata with
Spinach and Gruyère

Prosciutto with
Melon and Chives

Asparagus Vinaigrette

Kathie's Fruit Tart

Coffee and Espresso

Parmesan and Quince Skewers

This recipe was inspired by a cheese course offered at brunch buffets in many European cities.

CONNIE'S NOTES: *Quince paste (KWINTS) is a thick paste that tastes like a cross between apples and pears. It can be found in many grocery stores and in gourmet food stores, near the cheese section, and it can also be purchased online. Quince paste is very good with cheese, especially Parmesan and Manchego.*

Store any leftover quince paste in the refrigerator, and have it as a snack or a light dessert with a piece of cheese.

If you can't find hazelnuts, substitute almonds.

¼ pound chunk Parmigiano-Reggiano cheese cut into 1-inch cubes

About 2 ounces baby arugula leaves (¼ cup)

6 ounces quince paste, cut into 1-inch chunks

2 tablespoons honey

¼ cup toasted hazelnuts, finely chopped

Toothpicks

▶ Stack a Parmesan cube, several arugula leaves, and a chunk of quince paste on 12 small wooden skewers. Drizzle with honey and sprinkle with the hazelnuts. Serve at room temperature.

SERVES 4–6

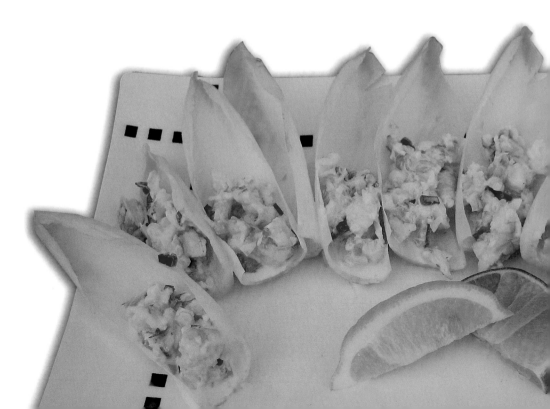

Shrimp Salad on Endive Spears

Cool and delicious, this appetizer needs to be made the night before so the flavors meld together. For a beautiful presentation, try to find both red and green endive at your grocery store or farmers' market. This appetizer would also be wonderful for a tea course.

CONNIE'S NOTES: *These salad shrimp can be found at many seafood counters.*

8 endive spears

³/₄ cup cooked baby shrimp, diced

1 jalapeño pepper, seeded and minced

¹/₄ teaspoon sea salt

¹/₄ teaspoon white pepper

Zest of 1 lemon

Zest of 1 lime

2 teaspoons fresh lemon juice

1 teaspoon fresh lime juice

1 shallot, minced

1 tablespoon mayonnaise or sour cream

▶ To prepare the endive, wash it, and remove any outer leaves that are bruised. Cut the bitter end off the bottom of the endive. Carefully separate the spears and lay them on paper towels to dry. Place in a resealable bag and refrigerate so they remain crisp. This process can be done a day in advance. Coarsely chop any leftover endive and use it in a salad.

▶ The night before: mix all the ingredients together except the mayonnaise, and refrigerate in a covered container. Just before serving, add the mayonnaise, and toss together.

▶ Place a rounded teaspoonful of the shrimp salad at the end of each endive spear, and serve immediately.

SERVES 4

Fava Bean Spread on Mini Toasts

If you can't find fresh fava beans, look for fava beans in jars or cans at Italian markets. Or you could substitute frozen green peas. Fava beans are delicious, be sure to order them when they are on the menu at your favorite restaurant.

CONNIE'S NOTES: *Fava (FAH-vuh) beans are a member of the pea family. They are a sure sign of spring in Italy. Sometimes, fava beans can be found in grocery stores during the spring months. They look like shriveled 3–5 inch brownish pods in the produce bin. Inside that thick pod is a white blanket covering a green bean.*

Shelling fava beans is a social occasion. It is similar to shelling the first fresh peas from the garden. This task is definitely worth the time and effort it takes.

2 pounds fava beans (about 1 cup shelled beans)

1 teaspoon kosher salt

1 clove garlic

2 tablespoons freshly grated Parmesan cheese

1 teaspoon fresh lemon juice

1 tablespoon extra-virgin olive oil

2 teaspoons fresh mint leaves

Salt and white pepper

▶ Remove the thick outer pods from the fava beans. Place the beans in a medium saucepan, barely cover with water, and add the salt. Bring to a boil, and blanch the beans for 3 minutes. Remove from the stove, drain the beans, set aside, and cool. When cool, remove the light green shell from the beans. It should slip off easily. There will be a bright green bean underneath.

▶ Place the garlic in a mini food processor, and mince. Add the cheese, lemon juice, olive oil, and mint and process until chunky. Check for seasonings, and then add salt and pepper to taste. Place in a covered container and refrigerate overnight.

▶ Serve with toasted baguette slices or mini toasts.

SERVES 4–6

Pomegranate and Pineapple Punch

This refreshing and different punch was inspired by the East Bank Club, a health club in Chicago. EBC serves it at their quarterly member appreciation days. Kids love this punch too, and it's also great for guests or family members who choose not to drink alcoholic beverages.

CONNIE'S NOTES: *If you want the punch less sweet, substitute club soda for the ginger ale. Also, you could substitute apricot nectar for the pineapple juice.*

1$^1/_2$ cups pineapple juice, chilled

1 cup pomegranate juice, chilled

2$^1/_4$ cups ginger ale, chilled

1 tray pineapple ice cubes made from 1$^1/_2$ cups of pineapple juice

Fresh pineapple for garnish

▶ Right before serving, pour the pineapple juice, pomegranate juice, and ginger ale into a punch bowl, and stir. Garnish with fresh pineapple chunks or the top of a fresh pineapple. Add the pineapple ice cubes.

SERVES 8–10 (SIX-OUNCE SERVINGS)

Breakfast Strata with Spinach and Gruyère

Strata is a fancy word for a custardy bread casserole that is served for brunch or breakfast because it can be made the day before. This is one of the best stratas I've tasted. It has lots of flavor, nice texture and crunch, and avoids some of the calories because meat is not included. This strata could easily be a quick weeknight supper with a salad and fruit. (Adapted from America's Test Kitchen)

CONNIE'S NOTES: *If you don't have Gruyère cheese, substitute different cheeses that melt easily and have lots of flavor, such as Asiago.*

6–8 slices Italian bread, 1 inch thick with crusts left on

1/2 stick (4 tablespoons) unsalted butter, softened

2 tablespoons finely chopped onion

4 green onions, finely sliced

10 ounces frozen chopped spinach, thawed and squeezed dry

1 teaspoon kosher salt

1/4 teaspoon white pepper

1/4 teaspoon freshly grated nutmeg

1/4 cup dry white wine

6 eggs, at room temperature

1 3/4 cups half-and-half

1/2 cup grated Gruyère cheese (about 4 ounces)

1/4 cup grated Parmesan cheese (about 2 ounces)

The night before serving

▶ Preheat the oven to 225°F. Put the bread in a single layer on a cookie sheet, bake for 15 minutes until dry, but not colored. Turn the bread over and bake for another 15 minutes. Cool. Butter one side of each slice of bread.

▶ Heat a medium skillet over medium heat, and add the remaining butter. Add both kinds of onions, and cook until soft. Add the spinach, 1/2 teaspoon of the salt, pepper, and nutmeg. Sauté for approximately 3 minutes. Transfer the mixture to a bowl and set aside to cool. Add the wine to the skillet, bring to a simmer, and reduce by half. Remove from the stove and cool.

▶ In a large bowl, preferably with a lip for pouring, whisk together the eggs, the remaining 1/2 teaspoon salt, half-and-half, and cooled wine. Set aside.

▶ Generously grease an 8-inch square baking dish with butter. Place half the bread, buttered side up, in the baking dish. Top with half the spinach, and half the Gruyère cheese. Top with the remaining bread, spinach, and Gruyère. Pour the egg mixture over the bread. Gently press the bread down so that the milk touches the bread on the top. Cover with plastic wrap, and refrigerate overnight.

The day you plan to serve the strata

▶ Remove the uncooked strata from the refrigerator and let stand at room temperature for 20 minutes.

▶ Preheat the oven to 325°F.

▶ Remove the plastic wrap. Top the strata with the Parmesan cheese. Bake, uncovered, until golden and puffed, 45–50 minutes. Remove from the oven and let the strata stand for 10 minutes. Cut into squares and serve .

SERVES 4–6

Kirk's Coffee

My husband Kirk makes the best coffee outside of Italy! His actuarial background comes in quite handy when making a cup of smooth, flavorful, and rich-tasting coffee.

He believes, like Italian baristas, that good water is the essential ingredient to great-tasting coffee. You may not have the best coffee grinder or coffeepot, but everyone has access to filtered water, either from your refrigerator, a filter on your tap water, or from bottled water.

He measures the water precisely and pours it into the appropriate coffee maker: press pot, drip, or espresso. He takes the fresh beans out of vacuum-tight containers, and grinds the beans to the appropriate grind for the coffee-pot. If your favorite coffee is espresso, you might want to invest in a burr grinder that can grind the coffee beans from coarse to fine. The grind of coffee is very important for espresso, because espresso machines force water over finely ground coffee with pressure. Otherwise, an inexpensive grinder will work just fine for drip coffee. You can also grind your beans at the grocery store or coffee store to ensure freshness. Just use the ground coffee within several days so that it is fresh. Very fresh beans are especially helpful when making espresso.

If you have a favorite restaurant that makes coffee, ask them what brand they use. In Chicago, many restaurants use Intelligentsia coffee, which is available to the general public.

Decide what your ratio is between ground coffee and water for the desired strength of your brew. Experiment with the measurements and record them until you get them just right. My husband makes fairly strong coffee by using one coffee scoop (or about two tablespoons of coffee) to 6 ounces of water. Then you will have the right proportions for that perfect cup of coffee every day. How do you like your coffee to taste: dark and sweet, bitter and creamy, burnt?

Keep all of your coffee apparatus together in one place: grinder, coffee maker(s), filters, liquid measuring cup with a lip, measurement tools, coffee scoopers, and tampers. My husband uses tiny brushes to keep the grinder free of residue. Make sure your coffeepot is very clean and also free of residue. Sometimes, a mixture of vinegar and water helps to keep the glass coffeepot meticulously clean.

While any coffeepot will work to brew coffee, glass containers that sit on the heat will eventually burn the coffee. Decide what's most important to you: having your coffee ready when you wake up, dishwasher safe, or storing the brewed coffee in a thermal type container. There are many good coffee websites on the Internet that discuss all the utensils you will need to make the perfect cup of coffee. My husband enjoys www.wholelattelove.com.

By all means enjoy this little bit of heaven every day!

Asparagus Vinaigrette

It is best to make this asparagus when it is in season, especially in the spring. Green beans could also be substituted for the asparagus. Add a soup or sandwich, and you have a light supper or lunch.

CONNIE'S NOTES: *Save the leftover asparagus ends for a homemade vegetable broth.*

³/₄ pound or 1 bunch asparagus, ends snipped off

1 teaspoon kosher salt

1 tablespoon diced red pepper

1 tablespoon diced yellow pepper

Vinaigrette

Juice of 1 lemon

Zest of 1 lemon

¹/₂ teaspoon kosher salt

¹/₄ teaspoon white pepper

1 tablespoon Dijon mustard

3–4 tablespoons grapeseed oil

▶ **The day before serving:** Fill a Dutch oven or large skillet about halfway with water. Add the salt, and bring to a boil. Add the asparagus, cover, and blanch for 3 minutes. Remove the asparagus from the boiling water, and place in an ice-water bath to stop the cooking process and to maintain the bright green color. When the asparagus is cool, transfer to paper towels and pat dry. Place the asparagus in a covered plastic container and refrigerate it overnight.

▶ **To make the vinaigrette:** In a small bowl, whisk together the lemon juice and zest, salt, pepper, and mustard, until the salt is completely dissolved. Slowly add the oil, and whisk until it begins to emulsify.

▶ Before serving, place the asparagus on a large platter. Sprinkle the peppers down the center of the asparagus, and drizzle with the vinaigrette. Serve.

SERVES 4

Kathie's Fruit Tart

My friend Kathie gave me this wonderfully easy recipe. Initially, I tried it with berries, but they became too mushy; sturdier fruits work better. This tart reminds me of the dump cakes my grandmother used to make with Jif cake mixes.

CONNIE'S NOTES: *Don't worry if you can't remove the bottom of the tart pan—sometimes it is very sticky. Just leave it and remember that when you are cutting the tart.*

To sprinkle on confectioners' sugar, use a mini tea strainer for a tidy application.

Crust

1 cup plus 1 tablespoon flour

1/2 teaspoon kosher salt

1/3 cup vegetable oil, plus enough water to make 1/2 cup total

Fruit

3–3 1/2 cups chopped fresh fruit such as rhubarb, apples, plums, nectarines, or peaches

Topping

1 cup sugar

1 stick (8 tablespoons) unsalted butter, melted

1 egg

1/2 teaspoon pure vanilla extract

▸ **To make the crust:** Gently mix the flour, salt, and oil together in a small bowl. Press into an ungreased 9-inch tart pan with removable sides. Set aside.

▸ Place the fruit on top of the unbaked crust. Set aside.

▸ Preheat the oven to 400°F.

▸ **To prepare the topping:** Mix the topping ingredients together in a small bowl. Pour over the fruit.

▸ Place the tart in the middle of the oven, and put a piece of aluminum foil on the rack below to catch potential drips. Bake for 55 minutes. If the tart browns too quickly, tent the tart with aluminum foil so it doesn't burn. Remove the tart from the oven, and cool for several minutes. Run a knife around the edge of the tart to loosen it. The tart will be very sticky. Let the tart cool completely.

▸ Remove the sides of the tart pan (remove bottom if you can do it easily). Place the tart on a serving platter. Serve at room temperature with confectioners' sugar, whipped cream, or a scoop of ice cream.

SERVES 8

This menu ushers in warmer weather with the rich, vibrant colors of the season: green, orange, red, and yellow. It is one of my favorite dinners because it combines all my favorite foods—cantaloupes, asparagus, salmon, and rhubarb—into a spectacular contemporary meal. It starts with a spicy red pepper dip and cools off with refreshing fruit soup served in shot glasses. The asparagus and sweet potatoes are the perfect accompaniments to grilled salmon. Finish off with an unusual rhubarb pie that has a meringue.

Although this menu is intended for the first cookout of the season, most of the ingredients can be found year round. Remember that the asparagus will be most flavorful in the spring and cantaloupes are the sweetest during the summer months. You can also make this meal inside using a grill pan and the oven.

Serve the soup right before the main course. The salmon and vegetables can be served family style so your guests or family can take just what they want.

Do you have any annuals such as petunias or daisies growing in your garden? Take a single flower and place it in a miniature bud vase at each place setting. (You can purchase these inexpensive bud vases at home décor stores.) If you have an elevated pie plate, set the pie on top of it and make it a celebration. When's the last time you and your family had a homemade pie? Enjoy the leftovers the next day, if there are any!

The Day Before

▶ **Make the soup, dip, and rub**

▶ **Prepare the crudités**

▶ **Make the piecrust dough**

▶ **Chop the rhubarb**

▶ **Prepare the sweet potato foil packets**

First Barbeque on the Deck

Roasted Red Pepper Dip with Crudités and Toasted Pita Bread

Aromatic White Wine (Viognier or Riesling)

● ● ●

Chilled Cantaloupe Soup

Prosecco

● ● ●

Cedar-Plank Salmon

Grilled Asparagus

Grilled Sweet Potatoes

Pinot Noir

● ● ●

Mom's Rhubarb-Meringue Cream Pie

● ● ●

Coffee

Roasted Red Pepper Dip

This dip has ingredients and flavors similar to those in romesco sauce, a classic Spanish sauce that is served with grilled fish and chicken.

1 pound (about 3) red bell peppers, halved lengthwise and seeded

8 large cloves garlic, unpeeled

4 tablespoons extra-virgin olive oil

2 medium plum tomatoes

1 cup whole almonds

2 teaspoons cumin seeds

1 tablespoon fresh lemon juice

1 teaspoon kosher salt

1/4 teaspoon red pepper flakes

1/4 teaspoon freshly ground black pepper

1 tablespoon hot water

Whole almonds, for garnish

▶ Preheat the oven to 500°F.

▶ Place the pepper halves, skin side up, and the garlic on a cookie sheet lined with parchment paper. Drizzle 2 tablespoons of the olive oil over the peppers and garlic cloves. Roast for approximately 20 minutes or until pepper skins are charred. You may need to turn the garlic cloves after 10 minutes to prevent burning. Remove and set aside.

▶ Reduce the oven temperature to 400°F. Place the tomatoes on a baking sheet. Spread the almonds and cumin seeds on the baking sheet in separate piles. Roast for 10 minutes or until the tomato skins split, almonds are toasted, and cumin seeds are toasted, but not burned.

▶ While the tomatoes are roasting, remove the skins from the peppers and garlic. Place both in a food processor. Add the roasted tomatoes, almonds, cumin, lemon juice, salt, red pepper flakes, and black pepper. Puree until smooth. With the machine on, add the remaining 2 tablespoons of olive oil and the hot water slowly through the feed tube. Check seasonings and add more if necessary. The dip should be rather thick, for dipping with crudités—such as endive, cucumber, and yellow pepper spears—and toasted pita bread.

SERVES 8

About Olive Oil

Extra-virgin olive oil is the result of the first pressing of the olives using the cold-press process. It is considered to be the fruitiest and finest of the olive oils. Extra-virgin olive oil can range in color from champagne to a greenish golden to a bright green. It is the most expensive of all olive oils. I prefer to use extra-virgin olive oil because of the flavor it adds to food. While taking a cooking class in Provence, I learned much more about using olive oil in cooking, and have been using it ever since. If you want to cook with a less flavorful oil, you might want to try virgin olive oil instead.

Many food stores have olive oil tastings. See which flavors you like best—they will vary from fruity to spicy, much like tasting different wines. You will notice that many olive oils come from the Mediterranean region, but California is also producing some very nice olive oils. Next time you go on a vacation to Italy, France, Spain, or Greece, be sure to buy some extra-virgin olive oil while you are there.

Don't forget about the health benefits of olive oil. Olive oil has a high content of monounsaturated fat that makes it a healthful dietary oil.

Chilled Cantaloupe Soup

This warm weather soup is refreshingly good. Make sure the soup is very cold by freezing part of the soup in ice cube trays, and placing a cube in each serving. The soup should be very thin and be drunk like a very cold beverage, in a small mug or shot glass.

Kaffir lime leaves can often be found in the produce section of gourmet food stores. If you can't find the leaves, just use the lime zest.

CONNIE'S NOTES: *For icy-cold soup, chill the soup mugs or shot glasses in advance by placing them in the freezer.*

Prosecco *(pro-SAY-co)* is a light white sparkling wine from Italy that adds a nice kick to the soup. It can also be drunk with appetizers in the summertime for a lighter, cheaper version of champagne.

³/₄ cup water

¹/₂ cup mint leaves

2 kaffir lime leaves

Zest and juice of 2 limes

2 medium cantaloupes

2 tablespoons honey

¹/₂ cup Prosecco sparkling wine

Slivers of fresh mint, for garnish

▷ In small saucepan, bring the water to a boil. Add the mint, lime leaves, and lime zest. Set aside off the stove, to steep for at least an hour to infuse the water with the additional flavor. Strain the mixture through a fine-mesh sieve (such as a tea strainer), squeezing out as much juice as possible. Discard the wilted mint leaves, lime peel, and leaves.

▷ Peel, seed, and coarsely chop the cantaloupe. Place half of it in the food processor and add the mint-lime water, lime juice, honey, and Prosecco. Process until smooth, and transfer the mixture to a large bowl. Process the remaining chunked cantaloupe, then mix it into the seasoned cantaloupe mixture. Check again for seasonings. Strain the soup through a fine-mesh colander into a plastic container. Discard the pulp.

▷ Freeze 2 cups of the soup in an ice cube tray. Cover and chill the remaining soup overnight.

▷ To serve, pour the soup into small mugs and add a cantaloupe ice cube. Garnish with slivers of fresh mint.

SERVES 6–8

Cedar-Plank Salmon

Cooking salmon on cedar planks gives it that cedar infusion that tastes so good. Since the planks are soaked, the salmon steams on the grill and stays very moist. The flavor and smell are heavenly. Your neighbors will like it too. You can buy untreated wood shingles very inexpensively at a specialty lumberyard. If you can't find them, cedar planks are available at gourmet food stores for about $10 each.

(Adapted from Palisades Restaurant in Seattle.)

Spice Rub

1 tablespoon paprika

1 tablespoon kosher salt

2 teaspoons freshly ground black pepper

1 teaspoon grated lemon zest

2 teaspoons brown sugar

1 teaspoon granulated garlic

1 teaspoon dried tarragon

1 teaspoon dried basil

Untreated cedar shingles

Four 5-ounce salmon fillets, bones carefully removed

▶ Combine all the spice rub ingredients in a mini food processor or mix by hand.

▶ Soak the shingles by placing them in a large rectangular cake pan or cookie sheet, cover with tap water, and weight the shingles down with wine bottles or canned food for at least 6 hours. Take the shingles out of the water right before you place them on the hot grill.

▶ Preheat a gas grill or prepare a charcoal fire.

▶ Place the salmon fillets on a platter and sprinkle approximately 1 teaspoon rub on each fillet, covering the surface. Let the salmon sit at room temperature for about 30 minutes.

▶ Place the salmon on the wet shingles and grill at medium heat with the grill lid closed. Grill for approximately 10–12 minutes for medium rare. Remove the salmon from the shingles and let them rest for approximately 5 minutes before serving. Discard the charred shingles.

SERVES 4; MAKES ¼ CUP RUB

CONNIE'S NOTES: *This spice rub will keep for several months if it is tightly covered to prevent drying out. The French call tarragon the "King of Spices". It can easily be found in the dried spice section of your grocery store.*

Cedar planks are safer to use in an oven than the thin wood shingles.

Always keep a small bottle of water with a sprayer close by the grill for flare-ups!

Grilled Asparagus

This is a very simple preparation for asparagus. For best results, use asparagus in season.

1½ pounds (approximately 2 bunches) medium-sized asparagus spears

2–3 tablespoons good-quality olive oil

Fresh lemon juice

Kosher salt

▶ Preheat a gas grill to medium or prepare a charcoal fire.

▶ Prepare the asparagus by snipping off the woody ends and rinsing. Pat dry. Toss with 2 tablespoons of the olive oil, and arrange on the grill. Grill on both sides until the asparagus begins to caramelize. Transfer to a serving platter, drizzle with lemon juice and the remaining tablespoon olive oil, sprinkle on kosher salt, and serve.

SERVES 4–6

Variation: To prepare the dish indoors, roast in a 400°F oven for about 20 minutes.

Grilled Sweet Potatoes

You won't believe how good the sweet potatoes taste, even with no marshmallows or brown sugar. The potatoes become very sweet during the grilling process—you will not need to add any butter or brown sugar. Maybe your kids will eat sweet potatoes all year round.

2 large sweet potatoes or yams, cut in half lengthwise

4 sprigs rosemary

Extra-virgin olive oil

▶ Preheat a gas grill or prepare a charcoal fire.

▶ Lay each sweet potato half on a piece of aluminum foil about triple the size of the potato. Lay a rosemary sprig on each sweet potato. Drizzle olive oil over each half and wrap completely in aluminum foil.

▶ Grill for approximately 30 minutes, the potatoes should be fork tender. Serve as an accompaniment to an entrée all year round.

SERVES 4

Variation: To prepare this dish indoors, bake the sweet potatoes in a 400°F oven for 30-45 minutes.

Mom's Rhubarb-Meringue Cream Pie

My mother made this pie when rhubarb was plentiful in the garden. Today, rhubarb is available much of the year, and you can make it anytime. I have adapted this recipe slightly to make it less sweet. It is more like a custard pie, than the usual rhubarb pie.

(Adapted by Connie Fairbanks)

CONNIE'S NOTES: *The volume of the meringue may be much lower on a high humidity day.*

Piecrust
1 cup flour

1/2 teaspoon kosher salt

1/3 cup plus 1 tablespoon vegetable shortening

2–3 tablespoons ice water

Filling
1/4 cup sugar

3 tablespoons flour

1 tablespoon fresh lemon juice

1/2 teaspoon finely grated nutmeg

1 tablespoon unsalted butter, melted and cooled

2 eggs, beaten

4 cups diced rhubarb (about 2 1/2 pounds)

Meringue
3 egg whites, at room temperature

1/4 teaspoon cream of tartar

6 tablespoons sugar

1/2 teaspoon pure vanilla extract

▶ **To make the crust:** In the bowl of a large food processor, pulse the flour and salt for a few seconds. Add the shortening, and process for about 15 seconds until it resembles coarse crumbs. Add the ice water 1 tablespoon at a time, pulse, and keep adding the water until the dough comes together. Remove the dough from the processor bowl, and form it into a disk about 6 inches in diameter. Wrap in plastic wrap and refrigerate it for at least an hour or overnight.

▶ With a lightly floured rolling pin and board, roll out the dough in a circle about 2 inches larger than a 9-inch pie pan. Place the dough in the pan, and flute the edges with the overhanging dough.

▶ Preheat the oven to 400°F.

▶ **To make the filling:** Stir together the sugar, flour, nutmeg, and butter in a mixing bowl. Add the eggs, and beat until smooth. Stir in the rhubarb. Pour the filling into the pie shell. Place the pie on a cookie sheet to catch possible drips. Bake for 15 minutes. Reduce the oven temperature to 350°F and bake for another 35 minutes, or until the center doesn't jiggle.

▶ Raise the oven temperature to 400°F for the meringue.

▶ While the pie is baking, make the meringue. Bring the eggs to room temperature by setting them out first thing in the morning. Beat the egg whites and cream of tartar together in a very clean glass or metal bowl (free of oil or residue) until foamy. Beat in the sugar 1 tablespoon at a time, continue beating until stiff and glossy about 4–5 minutes. Beat in the vanilla.

▶ Remove the baked pie from the oven, cool for a few minutes. Heap the meringue onto the hot pie filling and crust. Spread the meringue over the filling. Carefully seal the meringue to the edge of the piecrust to prevent weeping or shrinking. Bake for approximately 10 minutes, until the meringue is golden brown (watch carefully).

▶ Remove the pie from the oven and cool to room temperature. Then cover the pie and refrigerate it for several hours or overnight (preferably) to help the pie set up properly.

SERVES 6–8

If you polled your family on favorites, they probably would say let's have tomatoes, corn, chicken, and chocolate. This menu has all those ingredients and includes some surprises too: juicy chicken thighs with rosemary (instead of chicken breasts), and grilled corn kicked up with cayenne and lime juice. To finish, everyone can break off pieces of deep rich chocolate delights. This menu was inspired by a kitchen construction disaster, when I had no sink or water in the kitchen for a month. The meal can be made quickly and with a minimum of utensils and dishes. Picnic Anytime will cultivate memories of camping trips from your past with a few contemporary touches, such as the beverages.

Make the dinner simple, but also *special* by offering spa water at the beginning of the meal as an alternative to an alcoholic beverage. To make the simple refreshing spa water, halve several lemons and limes, and place them in a pretty water pitcher. Fill the pitcher half full with hot water and refrigerate it for several hours. The limes and lemons will infuse the water, imparting a fresh taste. You could use spears of cucumber in this water instead of the citrus. When you are ready to serve the water, fill the pitcher with ice, and serve this lightly flavored water.

Serve the potatoes and corn in their packets so your family or guests can open the packets themselves to keep everything hot. Serve the seasonal berries in a pretty glass bowl, or for a special touch, spoon them into wineglasses.

With this meal you want to pair a Chardonnay that is not too oaked. Also, a light red wine, such as a Pinot Noir, would match well with the grilled chicken. Finish the meal with a cup of espresso. Enjoy this special picnic anytime!

The Day Before

▸ **Marinate the chicken**

▸ **Prepare the corn and potato foil packets**

Picnic Anytime

Tomato Bruschetta

Rosé or Spa Water

▲ ▲ ▲

Rosemary-Marinated
Grilled Chicken Thighs

Hobo Potatoes

Grilled Spicy Corn

Chardonnay or Pinot Noir

▲ ▲ ▲

Fresh Seasonal Berries

Chocolate Delights

▲ ▲ ▲

Espresso

Tomato Bruschetta

Bruschetta *(broo-SKEH–tah)* are small Italian toasts that are a great way to start a meal. This recipe is best made when tomatoes are in season. If you want to prepare a platter of bruschetta in advance, do it just prior to serving or the bread will get soggy very quickly.

4 medium-sized tomatoes, seeded and diced

3 cloves garlic, chopped

2 tablespoons chopped red onion

1 tablespoon balsamic vinegar

Salt and pepper

1 tablespoon extra-virgin olive oil

Pinch of red pepper flakes

1 cup sliced fresh basil leaves

1 baguette, cut into ½-inch slices

1 whole garlic clove

Basil leaves, for garnish

▶ In a medium-sized bowl, combine the tomatoes, chopped garlic, onion, balsamic vinegar, salt and pepper to taste, olive oil, and pepper flakes and stir. Let the mixture sit at room temperature for at least 3 hours. At the last minute, stir in the basil.

▶ Preheat the oven to 400°F.

▶ Toast the baguette slices in the oven for about 10 minutes or grill until golden brown (about 2 minutes per side). Rub the slices with the cut side of the garlic clove, and drizzle olive oil over each slice.

▶ Serve the tomato mixture in a bowl, garnished with a small cluster of basil leaves. Let your family spoon it over the toasted baguette slices.

SERVES 4–6

Rosemary-Marinated Grilled Chicken Thighs

Once you try boneless, skinless chicken thighs, you may never eat chicken breasts again. Chicken thighs are very flavorful and remain juicy during the grilling process. Add additional rosemary sprigs to garnish the serving platter. This is the most flavorful chicken you will ever eat.

¼ cup fresh lemon juice

1 tablespoon olive oil

12 boneless, skinless chicken thighs (about 2½ pounds)

3 sprigs rosemary

▶ Preheat a gas grill to medium or prepare a charcoal fire.

▶ Whisk together the lemon juice and olive oil. Put the chicken in a resealable bag, and pour the marinade over it. Add the rosemary sprigs and refrigerate for at least 6 hours.

▶ Grill the chicken for about 10 minutes on each side, or until the juices run clear.

SERVES 4

Hobo Potatoes

This recipe will take you back to your Girl Scout days with "melt-in-your-mouth" comfort food potatoes. Don't forget the yummy crispies sticking to the foil! For a modern update from basic red potatoes, use creamer or fingerling potatoes.

Fingerling potatoes are the small, waxy potatoes that look like 2-3 inch fingers with a diameter of about 2 inches. They can be yellow, red, or purple. They are low in starch and great for roasting and in potato salads. Creamer potatoes are those small, yellow, new potatoes that can be found at most supermarkets.

1$\frac{1}{2}$ pounds fingerling, white creamer, or small red potatoes, cut into chunks

2 shallots or 1 small onion, chopped

Leaves from 8 sprigs fresh herbs, such as thyme, rosemary, or tarragon

2 tablespoons extra-virgin olive oil

4 tablespoons chicken broth

$\frac{1}{2}$ teaspoon kosher salt

$\frac{1}{4}$ teaspoon freshly ground black pepper

▶ Heat a gas grill or prepare a charcoal fire.

▶ Divide the potatoes among four 12x12-inch pieces of aluminum foil. Sprinkle the potatoes with the shallots and herbs, then drizzle $\frac{1}{2}$ tablespoon olive oil and 1 tablespoon chicken broth over each packet. Fold the foil around the potatoes to form the packet.

▶ Grill over medium heat for about 30 minutes on the top rack of your grill.

SERVES 4

Variation: To prepare this dish indoors, roast the packets in a 400°F oven for 40 minutes.

Grilled Spicy Corn

A favorite summer treat, this is a spicy alternative to the standard roasted corn on the cob. The recipe was inspired by the street vendors in the Indian section of Toronto.

4 ears corn, husked

2 tablespoons butter or olive oil

4 tablespoons fresh lime juice

1/2 teaspoon cayenne pepper

1/2 teaspoon kosher salt

▶ Preheat a gas grill or prepare a charcoal fire.

▶ Tear aluminum foil into four 12x12-inch squares and place an ear of corn on each square. Melt the butter in a small dish and stir in the lime juice, cayenne, and salt. Drizzle on each ear of corn. Wrap into a packet, and grill over medium- high heat for 30 minutes.

SERVES 4

Variation: To prepare this dish indoors, roast the packets in a 400°F oven for 40 minutes.

Chocolate Delights

When you just want one bite of chocolate, here's an easy-to-make confection that lets guests break off their own piece. This recipe was inspired by Avec Restaurant in Chicago.

CONNIE'S NOTES: *Good-quality chocolate is essential for this recipe! To chop the chocolate quickly, place it in a plastic bag, close it, and chop it with a wooden mallet.*

Paillette feuilletée (pa-YET-foo-YET-tay) are French wafers that have a crunchy texture. These wafers can be found only through a food distributor for restaurants, thus the substitute with rice cereal. Tara Lane, the former award-winning pastry chef at Avec and Blackbird in Chicago, says that crushed wafer ice cream cones would also be a good substitute.

10 ounces best-quality bittersweet chocolate, coarsely chopped

2 cups puffed rice cereal (non sugared), slightly crushed (or crushed wafer ice cream cones, or *paillette feuilletée* if you can find it)

▶ Melt the chocolate slowly in a double boiler, or a glass bowl placed over simmering water in a saucean. Remove the bowl from the simmering water, add the cereal, and stir. Quickly spread the mixture thinly on a piece of waxed paper. Let dry for several hours. Serve on a large platter and break off what you want.

SERVES 6–8

Summer in Chicago

Sometimes you need a menu for a quick light lunch for a charity meeting, or to celebrate friendships. You want a menu that can be assembled without a lot of fuss at the last minute, and here it is. Who said chicken salad has to be ho-hum and served on white toast? The star of this working lunch is a chicken salad made with chunks of pineapple, melon, and sweet red peppers. The salad is topped with a ginger-pineapple dressing, and banana bread is served alongside. Starting the lunch is a cold buttermilk soup with bay shrimp served in small mugs. Light mini desserts of apricots and dates finish the meal. (Do as the Europeans do and get back to work *after* lunch.)

Chances are this lunch will just be for women, so gather the pastel napkins and linen placemats. Use the china in that beautiful heirloom cabinet, and fresh flowers, such as small white roses or calla lilies. Do you have any flowers blooming in your garden? Keep the table décor fresh, light, and simple. Serve the dates and apricots on one of those beautiful antique plates from your grandmother, or on a wedding gift plate you've never used.

Brew the tea with fresh mint, and put out sugar cubes, and wedges of lemon for the "lemon squeeze." As told by my father-in-law, Alston, "Place the tines of a fork in the middle of a lemon wedge, and squeeze down the sides of the lemon." He guarantees that the fork keeps the lemon juice in your iced tea, not in someone's eyes!

The Day Before

▶ **Prepare the soup to meld flavors**

▶ **Bake the bread**

▶ **Make the pesto**

▶ **Poach and cube the chicken**

▶ **Wash and crisp the lettuce**

Working Lunch

Cherry Tomatoes with Pesto

●●●

Cold Buttermilk Soup with Shrimp

Pineapple Chicken Salad

Banana Tea Bread
Iced Tea with Mint and Lemon

●●●

Stuffed Dates

Chocolate-Covered Apricots

Cherry Tomatoes with Pesto

Basil pesto originated in Genoa, Italy. When you have that leftover basil at the end of the summer, make a batch of pesto. It can be used as a sauce for pasta, in white bean soup, on homemade pizzas, in appetizers, and on grilled fish. It is so easy to make, and the homemade version has a much more intense flavor than the store-bought variety. Toasting the pine nuts gives this pesto a unique flavor. Pestos can also be made with cilantro, parsley, and mint for other unique tastes.

CONNIE'S NOTES: *Pine nuts can be easily toasted on a cookie sheet in a toaster oven or in a conventional oven at 350°F, or in a skillet for several minutes. Pine nuts tend to burn quickly so watch them carefully. Cool and use as a garnish in pastas or appetizers.*

Pesto

2 cloves garlic

1/2 cup pine nuts, toasted

2 cups fresh basil leaves

1/4 cup freshly grated Parmesan cheese

2–4 tablespoons extra-virgin olive oil

12 small cherry tomatoes

1/4 cup toasted pine nuts, for garnish

▶ **To make the pesto:** Drop the garlic into a food processor with the motor running, and finely chop. Stop the motor, and add the pine nuts, basil, and Parmesan cheese, and process until chopped. With the motor running, slowly add the oil, processing until incorporated. Check for seasonings. Transfer the pesto to small plastic containers with lids and refrigerate. Pesto can be frozen in an ice cube tray for future use. Before using the pesto for pasta or appetizers, bring it to room temperature.

▶ **To prepare the tomatoes:** Using a small spoon, remove some of the seeds and pulp from the tomatoes so the cavity can be filled with pesto. Slice a thin section off the bottom of each tomato so that it will sit flat on a plate. Turn the tomatoes upside down onto a paper towel to catch the additional juices. Stuff each tomato with a scant teaspoonful of pesto and top with a toasted pine nut. Serve on a bed of basil leaves or toasted pine nuts.

SERVES 4; MAKES 1/2 CUP PESTO

Cold Buttermilk Soup with Shrimp

Great for a low-calorie, do-ahead lunch, this is a soup with a twist that can be made all year round. I like to serve each guest by placing the soup in a simple chilled glass pitcher and pouring it over the garnishes—it's a restaurant touch. This is great with a sandwich too!

CONNIE'S NOTES: *A **mandoline** (MAHN-duh-lihn) works very well for slicing cucumbers very thin. It is a hand-operated device with sharp adjustable blades that many chefs use for ultra-thin slices, fancy wedges, julienne cutting, etc. They can be found at home stores. If you decide to purchase a mandoline, get proper instruction on how to use it and how to protect your fingers and hands. Be sure that a hand guard is included with your purchase.*

$1/2$ seedless cucumber, peeled and coarsely chopped

1 shallot, cut into chunks

1 tablespoon minced fresh dill

1 quart low-fat buttermilk

2 teaspoons sea salt

$1/4$ teaspoon white pepper

$1/8$ teaspoon cayenne pepper

Garnish

$1/4$ very thinly sliced and seeded cucumber

$1/2$ teaspoon lemon zest

10 small cooked shrimp, deveined and cut into chunks

$1/2$ tablespoon fresh lemon juice

$1/4$ teaspoon sea salt

▶ Place the cucumber, shallot, salt, pepper, cayenne, dill, and 1 cup of the buttermilk in the bowl of a food processor. Process until pureed. Transfer to a bowl, add the rest of the buttermilk, and stir until mixed. Check for seasoning, and chill overnight in a covered container.

▶ Before you serve the soup, combine the garnish ingredients in a bowl and let stand for 15 minutes to meld the flavors. Distribute the garnish mixture among 6 soup bowls or small mugs. Pour the soup over the garnish and serve (the garnishes should float to the top).

SERVES 6–8

Pineapple Chicken Salad

This is not your ordinary chicken salad! It is very fresh and light with no mayonnaise. Use juicy chicken breasts, as they are the star of the salad! For a special twist, add some bay shrimp too.

CONNIE'S NOTES: *Use any leftover dressing with a fruit salad. This salad could be used for a picnic because there is no mayonnaise in the dressing. Take the dressing in a small jar, and toss it on the salad just before you serve it.*

Chicken

1 carrot

1 stalk celery

1 small onion, roughly chopped

2 whole chicken breasts (with bone in and skin on)

1 fresh bay leaf

1 lemon, sliced

1 teaspoon kosher salt

3 peppercorns

$\frac{1}{2}$ cup white wine

Dressing

$\frac{1}{2}$ cup pineapple juice

Juice of 1 orange

$\frac{1}{2}$ cup honey

1 teaspoon grated fresh ginger

2 shallots, finely chopped

$\frac{1}{2}$ teaspoon dry mustard

1 teaspoon kosher salt

$\frac{1}{2}$ teaspoon white pepper

$\frac{3}{4}$ cup vegetable oil

2 teaspoons fresh lemon juice

Salad

2 cups fresh pineapple chunks (1 pineapple)

12 small cherry tomatoes, halved

1 cup cantaloupe balls

1 cup honeydew balls

¼ cup diced celery

¼ cup diced green pepper

¼ cup diced red pepper

4 thinly sliced green onions, green and white parts

2 heads Boston lettuce, for garnish

▶ **To prepare the chicken:** Place the carrot, celery, and onion in the bottom of a medium-sized saucepan and put the chicken breasts on top of the vegetables. Add the bay leaf, lemon, salt, peppercorns, and wine. Just cover the ingredients with chicken stock or water, and turn the heat to high. (The chicken and vegetables should fit tightly in the saucepan.) Bring the liquid to a boil. Skim off the foam that forms on top, and discard it.

▶ Reduce the temperature to low and partially cover the pan. Let the mixture simmer gently until the chicken is finished cooking, about 60 minutes. Check for doneness by piercing the thickest part of the chicken breast, making sure the juices run clear.

▶ Remove the chicken from the pot and let it cool. Discard the bones and skin. If you aren't planning to use the chicken for a day or so, return it to the cooled broth and refrigerate. Strain the broth and use it in soups and for steaming vegetables. Cut the chicken into 1-inch chunks.

▶ **To make the dressing:** Combine all the dressing ingredients in a mini food processor or shake it in a jar. The honey will help to emulsify the dressing. Store in a tightly covered jar in the refrigerator. If the dressing separates, shake vigorously right before you serve it.

▶ **To assemble the salad:** Toss the chicken chunks and all of the salad ingredients, except the lettuce, together gently in a large bowl (this may be done in advance). Place lettuce leaves on six chilled plates. Distribute the tossed ingredients among the plates. Pass the dressing separately in a small pitcher, and let guests toss their own salad with the dressing.

SERVES 6; MAKES 2 CUPS DRESSING

Banana Tea Bread

This bread is as light as a banana cake, but you could eat it for breakfast too. It's also a great item to make for a bake sale.

CONNIE'S NOTES: *To get the volume in the mixture, make sure the eggs and butter have been left out for several hours. Pastry chefs use this trick all the time. Don't overbake the bread. Remember it continues to cook when you take it out of the oven. The mini loaves freeze very well for several months.*

If you have bananas that are about to be thrown out, mash them and then freeze them in a plastic bag or container, and use them later for bread, cake, and muffins.

1 stick (8 tablespoons) unsalted butter, at room temperature

$1^1/_3$ cups sugar

2 large eggs, at room temperature

$^1/_4$ cup sour cream

2 tablespoons light rum or whole milk

1 teaspoon almond extract

2 cups flour

$1^1/_2$ teaspoons baking powder

$^1/_2$ teaspoon baking soda

$^1/_4$ teaspoon salt

1 cup mashed ripe bananas

$1^1/_2$ cups chopped pecans

Confectioners' sugar

▶ Preheat the oven to 350°F. Grease and flour a loaf pan (4x9x2½ inches), 2 mini loaf pans (2x5½x3 inches), or mini muffin pans.

▶ In a large mixing bowl, cream together the butter and sugar until fluffy using an electric mixer. Add the eggs, sour cream, rum, and almond extract. Mix well. Sift together the flour, baking powder, baking soda, and salt. Add the dry ingredients alternately with the bananas to the butter-egg mixture, and mix until combined. Stir in the nuts.

▶ Pour the batter into the prepared pan. Bake for approximately 1 hour and 10 minutes, or until a toothpick comes out clean. Sprinkle with confectioners' sugar when cool.

MAKES 1 LARGE LOAF, 2 SMALL LOAVES, OR 30 MINI MUFFINS

Mini Pronto Desserts

These mini desserts taste decadent anytime with a cup of tea, and can be made in a matter of minutes. You won't feel guilty eating these.

Stuffed Dates

CONNIE'S NOTES: *Medjool dates are readily found fresh in most grocery stores, especially during the fall and winter months. This special variety of date is of superior size, succulent, has a meaty texture, and is delicious for a quick sweet. If you can't find them, use other plump dried dates that are not dried out.*

12 pitted Medjool dates

12 walnut halves

Confectioners' sugar for dredging

▶ Open the dates to remove the pits and place a walnut half in each date. Press the ends of the date together, roll in confectioners' sugar, and serve.

SERVES 4–6

Chocolate-Covered Apricots

CONNIE'S NOTES: *Chocolate is the star in this recipe. Look for quality bittersweet chocolate that is at least 60-65% cocoa.*

6 ounces bittersweet chocolate, chopped

12 dried apricots

▶ Melt the chocolate in a double boiler, or a small bowl over simmering water. Dip one end of each apricot into the melted chocolate, and set on a piece of waxed paper to dry for 2-3 hours.

SERVES 4–6

Bulots
Cuits
1kg 10,50€
Moules de
Bouchot
1kg 4,56€
Composez vous
même votre

Here's a twist on the traditional East Coast clambake of clams, corn, and potatoes served with a bib. My Midwest Clambake starts off with a tasty green olive spread, and then moves to the main event of grilled clams, scallops, mussels, shrimp, and spicy sausage served in a spicy broth. Tuscan bread is used to sop up all the flavorful juices from the seafood packets. To top off the meal, there is warm peach cobbler.

If you usually don't serve shellfish, this is a foolproof recipe that you and your family will enjoy. These seafood packets could be made on the grill or in the oven all year round. Purchase one of those small colored plastic buckets you might use for the beach, and use them for all the leftover shells. Put the bucket in the middle of the table so everyone can use it.

Pull out your favorite summery placemats and cotton dish towels instead of napkins. How about red, white, and blue for your color theme? Anchor some coordinating candles in quart canning jars with some sand layered on the bottom of each jar.

You would expect a white wine with shellfish, but since the seafood broth is spicy and Asian, a Riesling or a Sauvignon Blanc would be the best wine choices.

The Day Before

▶ **Make the tapenade**

▶ **Make the soup**

▶ **Make the watermelon ice cubes**

Midwest Clambake

Chunky Green Olive Tapenade
with Toasts

Watermelon Soup

Rosé or Champagne

▲ ▲ ▲

Tomatoes with Basil

Seafood Packets

Crusty Tuscan Bread

Riesling or Sauvignon Blanc

▲ ▲ ▲

Fresh Peach Cobbler

▲ ▲ ▲

Coffee

Chunky Green Olive Tapenade

Traditional black tapenade (ta-pen-AHD) is a thick paste made from capers, olives, anchovies, etc. It is used as a condiment in Provence. This green tapenade is quite different, but just as tasty. Serve green and black tapenades side by side for an unusual appetizer course. Since this tapenade is so easy to make, why purchase the jar version? The mini toasts are easily found in grocery stores. (Adapted from Patricia Wells' recipe)

2 cloves garlic

1 cup green olives such as picholine and cerignola, pitted

1/2 cup fresh basil leaves

2 tablespoons extra-virgin olive oil

Small bunch of basil, for garnish

▶ Chop the garlic in the food processor. Add the olives, basil, and olive oil. Process until chunky, but not pureed, just a few pulses. Transfer to a small bowl. Serve at room temperature with mini toasts. Garnish with a small bunch of basil. The tapenade can be stored in the refrigerator in a tightly covered container for up to a week.

Picholine *(pee-cho-lean)* olives are small, almond-shaped, light green olives from Nimes, France, in the Provence region. They have a fresh nutty flavor.

Cerignola *(chair-een-nyo-lah)* olives are very large, crisp green olives from Puglia, Italy, which is in the boot of the country.

Both types of olives can be found at gourmet food stores, or in many supermarket deli departments. Spanish stuffed olives should not be used in this recipe.

Watermelon Soup

This recipe was inspired by l'Etoile Restaurant in Madison, Wisconsin. The soup is sweet and savory, very thin, and very refreshing. Sometimes grocery stores have these miniature watermelons, or ask your produce manager to order one for you. Moscato and Prosecco are inexpensive, light Italian sparkling wines. Either will add a refreshing flavor and fizz to the soup. Enjoy the leftover wine as an apertif or as a dessert wine.

1/4 cup sugar

1 cup water

1 shallot, minced

4 basil leaves

4 mint leaves

1 miniature seedless watermelon (7 inch)

1 1/4 cups sparkling wine (such as Moscato d'Asti or Prosecco)

Pinch of salt

Basil leaves and mint leaves, for garnish

▶ Make simple sugar syrup by stirring the sugar and water together in a saucepan over low heat until sugar is dissolved. Bring to a boil, and add the shallot, basil, and mint. Set aside off the stove for at least an hour so the flavors can infuse into the sugar water.

▶ Cut the watermelon in half, remove any residual seeds, and cut off the rind. Dice 3/4 cup of watermelon and set aside. Coarsely chop the remainder of the watermelon and puree in a food processor with the sparkling wine. Pour the mixture through a fine sieve to separate the pulp from the juice. Discard the watermelon pulp.

▶ Strain the infused sugar water, and add it to the watermelon juice. Discard the basil and mint leaves and shallot. Add a pinch of salt, the reserved watermelon, and check seasonings. Freeze 2 cups of the soup in an ice cube tray. Chill overnight. Serve icy-cold in individual shot glasses or small mugs with a watermelon ice cube. Garnish with a small basil leaf and mint leaves.

SERVES 10

Tomatoes with Basil

Cherry tomatoes are very sweet in season. Look for the various colors and combine them for a fresh, quick salad.

CONNIE'S NOTES: *Use whatever small tomatoes are in season. In the wintertime, the cherry tomatoes in the mesh bags taste almost like fresh tomatoes. Use those if you would like to make this dish in the winter. If you go to farmers' markets, try to find red and yellow teardrop tomatoes.*

2 cups yellow and red cherry/teardrop tomatoes, cut in half
OR
1 each medium-size red, yellow, and green tomato, sliced

Kosher salt

Freshly ground black pepper

¹/₂ cup sliced fresh basil

2 tablespoons extra-virgin olive oil

▶ Place the tomatoes in a small bowl (or on a platter if using sliced tomatoes). Right before serving, sprinkle on the salt, pepper, and basil. Drizzle the olive oil over the tomatoes and gently stir. Taste for seasonings, and serve at room temperature.

SERVES 4

Seafood Packets

The flavors of these packets are wonderful. Use whatever seafood and sausage is available in your area. (Adapted from the *New York Times*)

CONNIE'S NOTES: *Purchase, clean, and serve the seafood on the same day if possible. Rinse the clams and mussels and debeard the mussels, if necessary, and remove any gritty materials. (The beard of a mussel looks like black steel and can be easily removed by pulling on the beard, and then discarding it.) Keep the seafood on ice in your refrigerator. If any of the clams or mussels are open, discard them immediately.*

Andouille *(an-DOO-ee)* is a heavily smoked French sausage.

Chorizo *(chor-EE-zoh)* is a pork sausage flavored with garlic and chili powder. It is used in Mexican and Spanish cookery.

Linguica *(lin-gwee-sah)* is a delicious Portuguese sausage that can be found in New England, and in the Newark, New Jersey area.

Andouille and chorizo can be found quite easily in the grocery store. These spicy sausages add a "kick" to the clambake.

32 mussels, cleaned and washed, beards removed

32 littleneck clams, washed

8 mahogany clams

8 jumbo shrimp, shelled and deveined

8 jumbo scallops

2 andouille, linguiça, or chorizo sausages, cut in half

2 tablespoons fresh minced ginger

1 tablespoon fresh minced garlic

1/4 cup chopped fresh cilantro

1/4 cup chopped fresh basil

1/4 cup chopped fresh mint

4 teaspoons soy sauce

1/2 cup dry white wine

2 tablespoons extra-virgin olive oil

2 limes, cut into eighths

2 lemons, cut into eighths

Lemon and lime wedges, for garnish

▶ Preheat a gas grill to medium or prepare a charcoal fire.

▶ Tear eight large pieces of extra-strength aluminum foil. Use two pieces as the base for each packet. Get all your ingredients ready to make an assembly line. Divide the shellfish among the four packets. Top each packet with the sausage pieces. Then add the garlic, ginger, and herbs. Splash on the soy sauce, wine, olive oil, and top with the lemon and lime pieces. Wrap the packets securely, and place on a medium hot grill. Grill for about 12 minutes with the grill cover closed.

▶ After grilling the seafood packets, discard any of the shellfish that do not open. Place the packets in large soup bowls. Let guests unwrap and dump their seafood and broth into their own bowl. Discard the aluminum foil. Serve immediately with crusty bread for sopping up the liquid.

SERVES 4

Variation: To prepare this dish indoors, put the packets in a roasting pan and bake for about 15 minutes at 450°F.

Fresh Peach Cobbler

Use only fresh peaches in this recipe or some other seasonal fruit like nectarines or plums. This cobbler contains more fruit than the usual cakelike cobbler. Serve plain, or with cream or ice cream.

Filling

4 pounds medium-ripe peaches, peeled, pitted, and cut into 1/2- 3/4- inch slices

1/2 teaspoon pure vanilla extract

1/2 cup sugar or less

1 tablespoon cornstarch

Topping

3/4 cup flour

3/4 cup sugar

1/4 teaspoon salt

1/8 teaspoon soda

1 1/8 teaspoons baking powder

2 large eggs

2 tablespoons whole milk

1/2 tablespoon orange juice

3/4 teaspoon pure vanilla extract

1/2 teaspoon almond extract

3 tablespoons unsalted butter, melted

▶ Preheat the oven to 325°F.

▶ **To make the filling:** Combine the peaches, vanilla, and sugar in an 8x8-inch glass baking dish. Let the filling sit for 15 minutes, or until the juices start running. Sprinkle the cornstarch over the top, stir, and bake until bubbly, or about 20 minutes.

▶ **To make the topping:** Sift together the dry ingredients in one large bowl. In another bowl, whisk together the eggs, milk, orange juice, and flavorings. Add the liquid mixture to the dry ingredients and whisk until smooth. Fold in the melted butter.

▶ Pour the batter over the hot peach mixture. Return the pan to the oven and bake until the cobbler is golden brown and a tester inserted in the middle comes out clean, about 35 minutes. Cool slightly and serve.

SERVES 6–8

This colorful and light summer menu brings together the best that summer has to offer. It starts with a spicy gazpacho, which is followed by grilled swordfish highlighted with oregano and pancetta, and then ends on a sweet note with a rustic fruit pie. Your family will appreciate all the lively flavors and multiple textures of this winner. Dry or slightly sweet Gewürztraminer *(guh-VURTS-trah-mee-ner)* is one of the few white wines that matches well with spicy or flavorful foods.

Even though this menu could be made all year round, the gazpacho and crostata taste best when vegetables and fruits are in season. Make it a family event and head to the farmers' market. What looks good? What smells good? On the way home you can the pick up the fish—ask the fishmonger what the best fish is today.

Don't forget to buy some fresh flowers at the market too. To welcome summer, pick up some sunflowers and some hot pink zinnias. To make a simple centerpiece, place wet floral foam in five-inch tin buckets and arrange the flowers simply.

Next time, serve the gazpacho and salad for a great healthy "on the road" lunch as a substitute for rest-stop food.

The Day Before

▶ **Roast the olives overnight**

▶ **Make the gazpacho**

▶ **Make the crostata crust**

▶ **Slice the garlic for orzo**

Summer's Finest

Roasted Olives

Gazpacho

Gewürztraminer

▲ ▲ ▲

Swordfish Kabobs with
Garlic Orzo

Grilled Tuscan Bread

Grape-Almond Salad

Pinot Noir

▲ ▲ ▲

Rustic Nectarine and
Blackberry Crostata

Roasted Olives

A restaurant in Boston inspired this dish. The roasting process enhances the flavor of the olives. The smell will permeate the air. To serve the marinated olives, insert colored toothpicks into a lemon or orange half. Let your guests help themselves, one by one.

CONNIE'S NOTES: *Use any leftover olives in a pasta sauce, and the oil in a vinaigrette.*

2 cups assorted green and black olives with pits, drained

3 sprigs thyme

3 sprigs rosemary

2 fresh bay leaves

8 cloves garlic

1 orange, cut into thick slices

1 lemon, cut into thick slices

1 cup extra-virgin olive oil

▶ Combine the olives, herbs, garlic, and fruit in a casserole dish. Cover with olive oil, and bake, covered, at 200°F for 8 hours, or overnight. Remove the herb sprigs and fruit. Serve at room temperature on a pretty flat dish.

SERVES 8–10

Gazpacho

Gazpacho (*gahz-PAH-choh*) is a cold and refreshing summertime soup from Spain. This recipe is an American version. In Spain, the soup is thickened with stale bread, and becomes a light pink color when all the vegetables are pureed. There, the chopped vegetable garnishes are served at the table, and placed on top of the soup. If you have any leftover soup, pack it for lunch the next day.

1 bunch green onions

3 tomatoes

1 cucumber, half roughly chopped, half diced

1 green pepper, half roughly chopped, half diced

1 jalapeño pepper, roughly chopped, including seeds

1 red pepper, half roughly chopped, half diced

2 cups loosely packed cilantro, including stems

4 cups low-sodium tomato juice

2 teaspoons kosher salt

1 teaspoon freshly ground black pepper

2 tablespoons extra-virgin olive oil

2 tablespoons balsamic vinegar

Juice of 1 lemon

Juice of 4 limes

$1/2$ teaspoon red pepper flakes

Cucumber spears, for garnish

▶ Cut all but 2 of the green onions into a few large pieces. Slice the remaining 2 and set aside.

▶ Place the tomatoes and all the chopped vegetables in a food processor, with 2 cups of the tomato juice, or as much as will fit into your food processor bowl and puree. Transfer to a large bowl, and add the remaining tomato juice. Stir the mixture. Add the reserved sliced green onions, the lemon and lime juices, the diced vegetables, and combine. Check for seasonings, especially for salt.

▶ Chill the soup in a covered container overnight so the flavors can meld together. Serve in chilled mugs with a cucumber spear.

SERVES 8–10

Swordfish Kabobs with Garlic Orzo

You could also use scallops, shrimp, salmon chunks, prawns, or any other fleshy fish for the kabobs. The orzo provides a nice base for the kabobs and is a nice change from potatoes or rice. Using the vinaigrette as a marinade and light dressing highlights the fish with a burst of citrus.

Pancetta *(pan-CHE-tuh)* is an Italian bacon that is cured with salt and spices, not smoked like bacon you find in the United States. You can find pancetta in the deli section of your grocery store and have them cut as much as you need. Sometimes, you can find pancetta prepackaged in the deli meats section. Pancetta adds so much flavor to pastas and vegetables. Compare the taste to bacon and decide for yourself.

Orzo is Italian pasta that you can find in a regular grocery store. It looks like large grains of rice.

Al dente *(al-DEN-tay)* is an Italian phrase meaning "to the tooth." There is a slight resistance when you bite into it; it's not soft or overdone.

Kabobs

8 thin slices of pancetta or 8 strips of bacon

2 pounds swordfish, rinsed and patted dry

Four 10-inch-long wooden or metal skewers

Lemon and lime wedges, for garnish

Oregano sprigs, for garnish

Vinaigrette

Juice of 2 lemons

Juice of 4 limes

$1/4$ teaspoon kosher salt

$1/4$ teaspoon freshly ground black pepper

4 tablespoons extra-virgin olive oil

2 teaspoons chopped fresh oregano

Orzo

2 tablespoons extra-virgin olive oil

4 cloves garlic, sliced

1 tablespoon kosher salt

$1^1/2$ cups orzo

Salt and pepper

▶ The pancetta is so thin that it does not need to be precooked. If using bacon, precook it in the microwave by placing the strips on a glass platter and cover with a paper towel to avoid splatters. Cook about 4 minutes on high until cooked, but not brown and crispy. Let the bacon cool and set aside.

▶ Remove the skin from the swordfish and cut the swordfish into 2-inch cubes to make kabobs. Thread each skewer with several pieces of pancetta and swordfish, interlacing the pancetta over each piece of swordfish. Make sure the whole strip goes around each piece of fish to add flavor and to keep the fish moist. Each skewer should have about 4 swordfish chunks and pancetta encasing each piece of fish.

- In a bowl, whisk together the vinaigrette ingredients.

- Place the kabobs in a rectangular cake pan in one layer. Pour half of the vinaigrette over the kabobs, and allow to marinate for about an hour, at room temperature. Reserve the rest of the vinaigrette as a dressing for the kabobs and orzo.

- Preheat a gas grill or prepare a charcoal fire. While the grill is heating, prepare the orzo.

- **To make the orzo:** Heat the olive oil in a 9-inch skillet. Add the garlic and sauté just until it turns golden brown. Be careful not to burn the garlic as it will become bitter. Set aside.

- Fill a medium saucepan about two-thirds full of water. Add the salt and bring to a boil. Add the orzo to the boiling water and cook for 5 minutes or al dente. Drain the orzo and add it to the garlic mixture in the skillet. Keep it hot in a bowl over simmering water. Add a little chicken stock if it gets dry.

- Grill the kabobs over medium heat, about 3–4 minutes per side.

- To serve, spoon the orzo onto a large serving platter, top with the kabobs, and drizzle the remaining vinaigrette over the kabobs. Garnish with lemon and lime wedges and sprigs of oregano.

SERVES 4

Grilled Tuscan Bread

My neighbors are from the Naples, Italy area. They serve this bread all the time, and shared their recipe with me. Delicious all year, indoors or out.

Ciabatta *(chyah-BAH-tah)* bread is firm white Italian bread with a thin, crisp crust and soft interior. Ciabatta means "slipper." The bread is wonderful for sandwiches too. You can find it at most bread markets, Italian delis, or simply ask for it.

1/2 loaf ciabatta bread or country bread, sliced 1 inch thick

1 clove garlic

Extra-virgin olive oil

Kosher or sea salt

▶ Grill the bread until golden brown on both sides or for about 2 minutes per side. Be careful not to burn. Remove from the grill or grill pan and rub both sides of the bread with a cut clove of garlic. Drizzle with olive oil, sprinkle on salt, and serve immediately.

SERVES 4

Grape-Almond Salad

Avec Restaurant in Chicago was the inspiration for this recipe. An unusual salad for any time of year, it is so simple, yet so good. Because the almonds are salted, no extra salt is necessary.

Marcona *(mar-coe-na)* almonds are very flavorful almonds from Spain. They have a richer more intense flavor than regular almonds. Marcona almonds can be found in the gourmet section of your grocery store.

1 cup seeded green grapes, cut in half

1 cup seeded red grapes, cut in half

1 cup Marcona almonds

1 cup flat-leaf parsley sprigs

2 tablespoons extra-virgin olive oil

▶ Lightly combine all the ingredients in a pretty bowl and serve at room temperature.

SERVES 4

Rustic Nectarine and Blackberry Crostata

A crostata (*crow-staw-ta*) is a simple Italian sweet. Crostatas need to look rustic and homemade, and not like a double-crusted American pie. Experiment using different types of seasonal fruits, like cherries and peaches.

(Adapted from *Bon Appétit*)

Turbinado *(tur-buh-NAH-doh)* sugar is raw sugar that has been steam-cleaned. The coarse crystals are blond colored and have a delicate molasses flavor. This sugar can be found in most grocery stores. You can also use this sugar for sweetening coffee and espressos.

Crust

1²/₃ cups flour

¹/₄ cup coarse cornmeal

3 tablespoons sugar

³/₄ teaspoon kosher salt

1 teaspoon grated orange zest

1³/₄ sticks (14 tablespoons) chilled unsalted butter, cut into ¹/₂-inch cubes

¹/₃ cup ice water

1 egg, beaten (for glaze)

2 tablespoons turbinado sugar

Filling

¹/₄ cup sugar, or to your taste

1 tablespoon cornstarch

4 medium nectarines, cut into 16 slices with peel left on

1¹/₂ cups blackberries

1 tablespoon fresh orange juice

¹/₂ teaspoon pure vanilla extract

▸ **To make the crust:** Combine the flour, cornmeal, sugar, salt, and zest in a large food processor and blend for 5 seconds. Add the butter, all at once, and pulse until it is reduced to pea-sized pieces. Add some of the ice water, and keep adding water until the dough just comes together into one piece. Don't overprocess the dough or it will become tough. Gather the dough into a ball, flatten into a disk, wrap it in plastic wrap, and refrigerate for at least 2 hours or overnight. Before rolling it out, let the dough sit at room temperature for about 5 minutes, or until it becomes pliable.

▸ **To make the filling:** In a bowl, mix together all the filling ingredients and let it sit for about 30 minutes or until the juices are released from the fruit.

▸ Preheat the oven to 375°F. Grease a 10-inch circle pan or pizza pan and line it with parchment paper.

▸ **To assemble the crostata:** Work quickly as the dough will become very soft, especially in the summertime. On a lightly floured work surface, roll the dough into a 10-inch circle or a shape that will fit the prepared pan. Transfer the dough to the pan.

- Spoon the filling into the middle of the dough, leaving about a 2-inch border of dough. Fold the edge of the dough in toward the fruit forming a crust about 4 inches wide. This outside crust should keep the fruit juices from leaking out. It doesn't have to be perfect. You will leave some of the fruit exposed in the center of the crostata. Brush the dough with the egg wash, and sprinkle on the turbinado sugar.

- Bake for 45–50 minutes until the crust is golden brown. If the crust starts to brown too quickly, tent it with aluminum foil. Cool for about 45 minutes, and serve with ice cream, cream, or plain.

SERVES 6

Oftentimes, you need a meal that you can prepare easily when people arrive. With this French-inspired menu, your friends and family can experience eating at a French bistro tonight. And you can remain stress free, because this is a meal you prepare and eat in stages.

Serve the radishes and tomatoes as appetizers while you are making the shrimp. Serve the sophisticated, but inexpensive kir as an aperitif *(ah-pehr-uh-TEEF)* just like they do in France. Aperitifs are nothing more than light alcoholic drinks taken before lunch or dinner. Other aperitifs could include: champagne, sherry, or Dubonnet.

While your guests are eating the shrimp at the kitchen counter, prepare and bake the *gougère,* and open the wine to let it breathe. Mix the dressing for the salad in a separate bowl. Place the greens in a large salad bowl. Toss the salad, and serve the main course, the *gougère,* hot out of the oven at the dining room table. Serve them quickly, as they will deflate immediately. Pass the salad and pour the wine.

Since the menu is casual, I make a decadent, but light torte to go with the somewhat heavy and filling *gougère.* If you have a deck or a porch, go sit and have dessert and coffee there. Send any leftover dessert home with your friends.

A votre santé!

The Day Before

▶ **Clean the radishes and lettuce**

▶ **Roast the tomatoes**

▶ **Make the torte and sauce**

Book Club Supper

French Breakfast Radishes
with Butter and Kosher Salt

Roasted Plum Tomatoes
with Goat Cheese

▰ ▰ ▰

Kir

Spicy Shrimp

▰ ▰ ▰

Savory *Gougère*

Green and White Salad

Red Burgundy or Rhône Wine

▰ ▰ ▰

Aunt Della's Raspberry-Pecan Torte

▰ ▰ ▰

Coffee

French Breakfast Radishes with Butter and Kosher Salt

I first had these radishes with my friend, Anne, in Limoges, France. She served them as part of a picnic lunch. They were so delicious that my husband and I have been hooked on them for five years. We find these tiny French pink and white radishes at the farmers' market. You can also use radishes that you find at your local grocery store.

2 small bunches French breakfast radishes, washed and stemmed

3 tablespoons kosher salt

1/2 stick (4 tablespoons) sweet butter, flattened into a pat, at room temperature

▶ Make three piles of the radishes, salt, and butter on a serving plate. Let your guests help themselves by dipping the radishes in the butter and then the salt.

SERVE 4-6

Roasted Plum Tomatoes with Goat Cheese

They taste like summer's best tomatoes! The sweet, concentrated flavor of the tomatoes is a great contrast to the herbed goat cheese mixture. Use these roasted tomatoes for appetizers, pasta sauces, and salads.

CONNIE'S NOTES: *The tomatoes will shrivel and reduce in size by at least a third because the moisture evaporates with the slow roasting.*

2 pounds (about 12) smallish plum tomatoes, cut in half lengthwise

3 cloves garlic, minced

1/2 teaspoon kosher salt

1/4 teaspoon freshly ground black pepper

2 tablespoons extra-virgin olive oil

4 ounces plain goat cheese

Extra-virgin olive oil

Freshly minced herbs such as flat-leaf parsley, thyme, tarragon, or sliced basil leaves

▶ Preheat the oven to 200°F. Line a cookie sheet with parchment paper.

▶ Sprinkle the tomatoes with the garlic, salt, and pepper. Drizzle with the 2 tablespoons olive oil, and bake, uncovered, for 3½–4 hours. Let the tomatoes cool.

▶ Place approximately 1–2 teaspoons of cheese on each tomato. Sprinkle with the herbs and drizzle with a small amount of olive oil. Arrange on a plate garnished with additional herbs, and serve.

SERVES 4–6

Kir

Kir *(keer)* common aperitif around Lyon, France. It is Aligoté *(a-li-go-TAY)* wine poured with crème de cassis, a black currant liqueur. Aligoté is a dry white burgundy. It is very inexpensive (about $6 a bottle) compared to champagne and can be found at many liquor stores. If you want to make kir royale, just use champagne instead.

Approximately ½ cup crème de cassis liqueur

1 bottle Aligoté wine, chilled

Strips of lemon zest

▶ Put one part crème de cassis in the bottom of a champagne glass and add 4 parts of Aligoté. Top with a thin piece of lemon zest. Serve.

SERVES 4–6

Spicy Shrimp

A zesty shrimp appetizer that's easy to do on a grill or on top of the stove.

CONNIE'S NOTES: *Sweet smoked paprika can be found in specialty stores and via the Internet. It is a unique and versatile Spanish seasoning that can be used in stews, on vegetables (especially Swiss chard), and with potatoes and chicken.*

2 tablespoons extra-virgin olive oil

¹/₂ teaspoon red pepper flakes

4 cloves garlic, finely chopped

12 jumbo shrimp, cleaned and deveined

2 teaspoons sweet smoked paprika

Sea salt

1 lemon, half for juice, half cut into wedges

▶ In a large skillet, heat the olive oil and red pepper flakes together for several minutes, until very hot, but not smoking. Add the garlic, and sauté for 30 seconds. Add the shrimp and paprika, and toss until the shrimp turn pink, about 2–3 minutes. Serve immediately on a deep platter, pouring the garlic and olive oil over the shrimp. Sprinkle with sea salt and drizzle with lemon juice. Garnish with additional lemon wedges.

SERVES 4

Variation: To serve the shrimp as an appetizer, place round toothpicks into a half lemon and serve alongside the mound of shrimp.

Savory *Gougère*

A meal by itself with a glass of wine! *Gougère (goo-ZHAIR)* **is a cream-puff-like savory pastry served as an appetizer in the Burgundy region of France. With the addition of cheese to the top, the** *gougère* **will have a crispy exterior before you bite into the next layer of cheesy pastry. If you are good with a pastry bag, you could pipe the dough into individual puffs instead of a ring.**

CONNIE'S NOTES: *Gruyère is a Swiss or French cow's milk cheese with a rich, sweet, nutty flavor.*

Experiment using different fresh herbs to make this a savory pastry.

1 cup water

1 teaspoon kosher salt

¼ teaspoon freshly ground black pepper

½ teaspoon dry mustard

Pinch freshly grated nutmeg

1 stick (8 tablespoons) unsalted butter

1 cup flour

1 teaspoon Dijon mustard

2 tablespoons chopped tarragon leaves

1½ cups shredded Gruyère cheese

4–5 large eggs, at room temperature

Egg wash (1 egg and 1 teaspoon cream whisked together)

▶ Preheat the oven to 400°F. Butter a piece of parchment paper that will fit a 13–14 inch pizza pan.

▶ In a medium saucepan, combine the water, salt, pepper, dry mustard, nutmeg, and butter and bring to a boil over medium heat. Remove from the stove, and quickly stir in the flour until the mixture comes together. Return to low heat and keep stirring until the dough almost forms a ball, about 2 minutes.

▶ Remove from the stove, and add the Dijon mustard, tarragon, 1 cup of the cheese, and the eggs (one a time) beating vigorously with an electric mixer. You may need only four eggs, depending on the size of the eggs. The mixture should be glossy, without the dough becoming too runny.

▶ With a tablespoon, drop the dough in small mounds (of about 2 inches) in a circle onto the prepared pan. The dough mounds should touch each other, forming a ring. Brush the pastry with the egg wash, and sprinkle with the remaining ½ cup cheese.

▶ Bake for 15–20 minutes, or until the *gougère* is golden brown and puffed. Serve immediately as it will deflate quickly, just like a soufflé. When the *gougère* has cooled slightly, just use your hands to break it into pieces.

SERVES 4 AS AN ENTRÉE, 6–8 AS AN APPETIZER

Green and White Salad

An unusual salad with lots of crunch and textures, this is refreshing, light, and tastes great with food during the harvest season. Luckily, the ingredients are available all year long! The dressing could be used as a light citrus dressing for many vegetables, salads, and fruit salads.

CONNIE'S NOTES: *Grapeseed oil is a nice alternative to extra-virgin olive oil. It is light, nutty, and enhances the natural flavors of food because it has a neutral flavor.*

Frisée *(free-ZAY)* is a member of the chicory family and is often seen in mesclun mix. The leaves are curly, have a mildly bitter flavor, and range from yellow-white to yellow-green in color.

Salad

1/2 medium bulb fennel, thinly shaved, fronds reserved

2 medium Granny Smith apples, thinly sliced and sprinkled with lemon juice

4 stalks celery, thinly sliced

1/2 head frisée, torn

1/2 head Bibb lettuce, torn

1 endive, sliced

1/2 cup flat-leaf parsley leaves (discard stems)

Dressing

Juice of 1 lemon

Juice of 1 lime

3 tablespoons honey

1 teaspoon sea salt

1/4 teaspoon white pepper

5 tablespoons grapeseed oil

▶ Place all the salad ingredients in a salad bowl, and refrigerate.

▶ **To make the dressing:** Whisk together the juices, honey, salt, and pepper in a small bowl. Slowly add the oil and whisk together until it emulsifies. Place the dressing in the refrigerator until you plan to use it. If the dressing separates, just give it a good shake before you pour it over the salad.

▶ When you are ready to serve the salad, pour over just enough dressing to lightly coat the salad. Toss and serve immediately.

SERVES 4–6

Aunt Della's Raspberry-Pecan Torte

My aunt always made this for special occasions, but why wait? This is a light dessert that serves a crowd. For a restaurant touch, you can use a squirt bottle to garnish the individual dessert pieces with the raspberry sauce and dust with confectioners' sugar.

CONNIE'S NOTES: *It's easy to dust a small surface with confectioners' sugar if you use a small tea strainer as a small sifter.*

Torte

1¼ cups flour

⅓ cup confectioners' sugar

1 stick (8 tablespoons) unsalted butter, at room temperature

Two 10-ounce packages frozen raspberries, thawed, drained, juice reserved

1 cup chopped pecans

2 eggs

1 cup granulated sugar

½ teaspoon salt

½ teaspoon baking powder

1 teaspoon pure vanilla extract

Sauce

½ cup water

½ cup sugar

2 tablespoons cornstarch

Reserved raspberry juice

1 tablespoon fresh lemon juice

▸ Preheat the oven to 350°F.

▸ **To make the torte:** Combine 1 cup of the flour, the confectioners' sugar, and butter. Using your hands, press these ingredients into a 9 x 13-inch pan. Bake for 15 minutes, or until golden brown. Cool and set aside.

▸ Spoon the berries over the cooled crust, and sprinkle with the nuts. In a medium bowl, beat together the eggs and sugar until fluffy. Add the salt, the remaining ¼ cup flour, baking powder, and vanilla. Blend until smooth. Pour the batter over the nuts and berries. Bake for 30 minutes or until golden brown. Cool.

▸ **To make the sauce:** In a medium saucepan whisk together the water, sugar, cornstarch, and raspberry juice over medium heat. Stir until slightly thickened. Remove from the stove and stir in the lemon juice. Let cool.

▸ To serve, cut into squares and serve with whipped cream or ice cream, and the raspberry sauce.

SERVES 12–16

Every once in a while serving a menu that's off the beaten path is fun. A new menu helps prevent, "Are we having this again?" Unless you live in Miami or New York City, you probably have not tasted Cuban food. The Cuban culture is a melting pot from the Spanish, French, African, Arabic, Chinese, and Portuguese cultures. This menu should stimulate you and your family to try delicious Cuban food, and enjoy it. The meal starts spicy and stays spicy until the end. Mojitos pair well with the appetizers of jicama sticks and black bean salsa and chips. The pork tenderloin says Miami with the flavor boosters of oregano, cumin, lime, and orange. To cool down, dessert is grilled plums with ice cream and Cuban coffee.

Serve the chips in wicker baskets lined with brightly colored napkins. Put out some tropical flowers such as orchids or birds of paradise, or cut some bright orange and pink Gerbera daisies for the table. Do you have any lime green, turquoise, or pink placemats and napkins? Do you have any of those wooden watermelon plates that someone gave you, and you've never used? Use them all to set the festive mood.

Top off the meal with a Cuban coffee, which is nothing more than strong espresso with a lot of sugar, according to my Cuban sister-in-law, Alicia. This coffee is about double the strength of American coffee. The Cubans know this coffee as a "shot" or a "jolt." To-go cups of Cuban coffee are available in thimble-sized paper cups all around Miami. To learn more about Cuban cuisine, try some coffee and a Cuban sandwich at the Miami International Airport!

Salud!

The Day Before

- **Make the salsa**
- **Roast the vegetables for the salad**
- **Marinate the pork**

Miami Heat

Black Bean Salsa and Chips

Spicy Jicama Sticks

Mojitos

• • •

Grilled Cuban Pork Tenderloin

Orzo and Roasted Vegetable Salad

Dry Riesling or Pinot Noir

• • •

Grilled Plums with Thyme and Vanilla Ice Cream

• • •

Cuban Coffee

Black Bean Salsa

Fresh and spicy anytime, this very tasty appetizer is also low in calories. You could also double the ingredients and serve it as a salad.

One 15.5 ounce can black beans, drained and rinsed

1 mango, peeled, seeded, and chopped

1 jalapeño pepper (ribs and seeds removed), chopped

1/2 cup lightly chopped cilantro leaves

1/2 cup chopped red onion

1/2 cup chopped sweet red pepper

1/2 cup chopped yellow pepper

1/2 teaspoon freshly ground black pepper

1/2 teaspoon ground cumin

1/2 teaspoon kosher salt

Juice of 4 limes

2 tablespoons extra-virgin olive oil

Cilantro sprigs, for garnish

▶ Mix together all the ingredients in a bowl, and let flavors meld together for several hours. Serve at room temperature with red, white, blue, and yellow corn chips. Garnish the salsa with sprigs of cilantro.

SERVES 4–6

Spicy Jicama Sticks

Jicama **(HEE-kah-mah)** is a root vegetable that looks like a large potato. It is slightly sweet, very crisp, and wonderful as an appetizer to nibble on.

Half a 4-inch Jicama

$^1/_2$ cup fresh lime juice (about 8 limes)

$^1/_2$ teaspoon (or more) chili powder

▶ Peel the jicama and cut half of it into matchstick pieces about 6 inches long by 1 inch thick. Place in a bowl, and save the rest for another snack.

▶ Whisk together the lime juice and chili powder to taste. Pour the marinade over the jicama and let sit at room temperature for at least an hour. Place the spears in a festive glass and let your family help themselves.

SERVES 4

Mojitos

Mojitos (mo-HEE-toes) are the Cuban cousin to the traditional American mint julep. They have been enjoyed in Miami for years, and are slowly making their way north. It has been said that Ernest Hemingway enjoyed mojitos in Havana. Fresh mint is a must!

3 slices lime

6 fresh mint leaves

2 teaspoons sugar

$1^1/_2$ ounces rum

$^1/_2$ cup crushed ice

Club soda

▶ In a tall thin glass, combine the lime, mint, and sugar. Muddle or mash together until the lime slices start releasing their juice and the mint leaves look tattered. Add the rum, scoop in the ice, cover, and stir. Top with a splash of club soda. If you like, add a sprig of mint or a lime slice for a garnish. Enjoy!

SERVES 1

Grilled Cuban Pork Tenderloin

This is one of the most tasty pork tenderloins you will make. My Cuban sister-in-law asked for this recipe so I knew it was a hit! If you are in Miami, use sour oranges that are readily available.

(Adapted from *The Chicago Tribune*)

CONNIE'S NOTES: *Sour oranges are smaller than navel oranges and they have a more sour taste. If you can find them, be sure and add the lime juice too. Do not overcook the pork; tenderloins cook very quickly and will dry out. While meat is resting, it keeps cooking.*

6 cloves garlic

1 tablespoon kosher salt

1 tablespoon ground oregano

1 tablespoon freshly ground black pepper

2 pork tenderloins, about 1 pound each

Juice of 2 oranges and 2 limes, and wedges for garnish

Oregano sprigs, for garnish

▶ Mash the garlic, salt, oregano, and pepper into a paste, or pulse in a food processor. Place the pork in a glass dish. Rub the paste over the pork and let it soak in for 30 minutes. Transfer the pork to a ziplock bag, and add the orange and lime juices. Seal the bag and refrigerate for at least 4 hours or overnight.

▶ Preheat a gas grill, or prepare a charcoal fire.

▶ Remove the pork from the refrigerator, and let it sit for at least 30 minutes or until room temperature. Place the tenderloins on a medium grill, and pour the marinade over. Watch for flare-ups. Grill until medium rare, or about 6 minutes per side. Remove the pork from the grill and let it rest for at least 10 minutes. Slice and serve. Garnish with orange and lime wedges, and sprigs of fresh oregano.

SERVES 4

Variation: You could also prepare these tenderloins in a grill pan on top of the stove, and finish them in a 350°F oven for about 6 minutes.

Orzo and Roasted Vegetable Salad

Guests rave about this salad because of the fresh flavors and textures. It appears complicated, but it is not. This is great for a group of people, and those with vegetarian tastes. Leftover salad is great for lunch the next day!

Vegetables

1 small eggplant, cut into 1-inch chunks

1 red bell pepper, cut into 1-inch chunks

1 yellow pepper, cut into 1-inch chunks

1 orange pepper, cut into 1-inch chunks

1 red onion, cut into 1-inch chunks

4 cloves garlic, minced

$1/3$ cup extra-virgin olive oil

$1 1/2$ teaspoons kosher salt

$1/2$ teaspoon freshly ground black pepper

Orzo

1 cup orzo

1 tablespoon kosher salt

Dressing

$1/3$ cup fresh lemon juice (2 lemons)

$1/3$ cup extra-virgin olive oil

Zest of 1 lemon

Last-minute ingredients

6 scallions (white and green parts) sliced

$1/4$ cup toasted pine nuts

$1/2$ pound feta cheese, diced

15 fresh basil leaves, sliced

▶ **To roast the vegetables:** Preheat the oven to 400°F. Toss together all the vegetable ingredients in a large bowl. Place on a large sheet pan lined with parchment paper. Roast for about 40 minutes, turning several times. Set aside to cool.

▶ **To prepare the orzo:** Fill a medium saucepan about two-thirds full of water and add the salt. Bring to a boil, add the orzo, stir, and cook until al dente or about 12 minutes. Drain, and set aside to cool for about 10 minutes.

▶ **To prepare the dressing:** Whisk together the dressing ingredients in a small bowl and set aside.

▶ **To assemble:** Place the roasted vegetables in a large bowl, add the slightly cooled orzo and the dressing, and stir lightly. (It's important to add the dressing to the warm orzo so that the dressing is absorbed.) Add the scallions, pine nuts, and cheese. Check for seasonings. Toss lightly. Let sit at room temperature for several hours. To serve add the basil leaves, and toss. Garnish with additional basil leaves.

SERVES 8–10

Grilled Plums with Thyme and Vanilla Icream

A very simple dessert. Experiment using different seasonal fruits such as nectarines or peaches, and different herbs such as fresh rosemary or mint. It's important that the fruit is firm, otherwise, it will get very mushy on the grill. If you want to keep it low calorie, eliminate the ice cream.

½ cup honey

1 tablespoon fresh thyme leaves

1 tablespoon balsamic vinegar

4 large or 8 small plums, pitted and cut in half

Thyme sprigs, for garnish

Vanilla ice cream (optional)

‣ Mix together the honey, thyme, and vinegar in a small bowl. Let sit for several hours so the thyme can infuse into the honey.

‣ Preheat a gas grill to medium or prepare a charcoal fire. Brush the plums with the honey mixture. Grill for about 3 minutes on each side.

‣ Remove the plums from the grill, and divide them among four small dessert plates. Garnish with thyme sprigs, and add a small scoop of vanilla ice cream. Drizzle leftover honey over each dessert, and serve.

SERVES 4

FALL & WINTER
MENUS

What a wonderful meal to usher in the season with all the flavors of autumn. Earthy mushrooms are served with toasts, followed by a one-plate main course featuring a pork chop served atop a bed of squash, leeks, apples, and tiny sugar tomatoes. Finish the meal with an old-fashioned apple cake and a few chocolates. Make a trip to the farmers' market with your kids, and see what looks good, just like the chefs do. Find those Honey Crisp apples and those beautiful leeks, taste the sweet grapes and tiny grape tomatoes. Ask the vendors at your favorite stand about any new varieties of squash. Smell those fragrant bunches of sage, basil, and thyme for a dollar each. Then go home and cook! If you go to the market on a weekly basis, you will begin to know the vendors and they will recognize you.

Why not set your fall table with some new royal blue placemats and coordinating striped napkins of rich orange, blue, and burgundy? Pick up some tiny pumpkins and place them by each place setting to add a dash of fall color.

Have you been drinking a lot of Pinot Noir the past year because it pairs well with so many foods? Why not try a Riesling instead? There are two types of Riesling wines: dry and sweet. For this menu you will want to go with a dry Riesling—it goes very well with the pork.

It seems that just about everyone loves a small bit of chocolate at the end of the meal. If someone has given you nice chocolates, arrange them on one of your small beautiful glass plates.

Celebrate a new season—fall. Cheers!

The Day Before

▶ **Make the cake**

▶ **Peel and chop the squash**

▶ **Slice the leeks**

Fall Feast

Sautéed Mushrooms on Toasts

Champagne or Sparkling Wine

• • •

Pork Chops with Savory Fruit Sauté
on Squash Puree

Pinot Noir or Riesling

• • •

Elegant Apple Cake

Assorted Chocolates

• • •

Coffee

Sautéed Mushrooms on Toasts

Wonderful earthy flavors for a fall appetizer. Serve it in a martini glass for a special touch.

CONNIE'S NOTES: To clean mushrooms, just wipe them off with a paper towel or rinse them quickly. Do not soak them in water as they are already mostly water. Try using whatever interesting mushrooms are available at your grocery store. They all have earthy flavors and textures.

The mushroom sauté could be served with toast points and a small green salad as a salad course.

2 tablespoons extra-virgin olive oil

1 small onion, thinly sliced

1/2 cup roughly chopped shiitake mushrooms

2/3 cup roughly chopped Portobello mushrooms

2 cups sliced white mushrooms

1 tablespoon chopped fresh sage

1 tablespoon sliced fresh basil

1 1/2 teaspoons fresh thyme leaves

1/2 teaspoon kosher salt

1/4 teaspoon freshly ground black pepper

1/4 cup dry red wine

1 tablespoon tomato paste

1 tablespoon unsalted butter

6 thin slices white bread or brioche, crusts removed

▶ Heat a medium skillet over medium heat. Add the olive oil and onion and sweat the onion until soft. Add the mushrooms, herbs, salt, and pepper, and sauté until soft. Deglaze the pan by adding the wine and tomato paste, and reduce until the liquid is almost evaporated. Check for seasonings, and stir in the butter.

▶ Toast the bread and cut into triangles.

▶ Serve the mushrooms in a large martini glass garnished with some of the fresh herbs. Place a plate under the martini glass, and serve with toasted bread triangles.

SERVES 4–6

Pork Chops with Savory Fruit Sauté on Squash Puree

This menu was inspired by a cooking class with Paul Kahan, owner of Blackbird Restaurant in Chicago, and James Beard Midwest Regional Winner for Best Chef 2004. We went to the farmers' market and were inspired by the seasonal ingredients available that day. The combination of the flavors of this entrée is wonderful and so healthy. Paul believes quality entrées happen if you season "as you go" and use the freshest ingredients possible!

CONNIE'S NOTES: *Paul is beginning to use a lot more grapeseed oil in his restaurant because it is lighter than olive oil, and you can heat it to very high temperatures. See what you like better in your own home cooking!*

2 tablespoons grapeseed oil

3 leeks, thinly sliced, white parts only

2 Granny Smith or Honey Crisp apples, thinly sliced

Kosher salt and freshly ground pepper

4 bone-in pork chops, 1¹/₂–2 inches thick

All-purpose flour for dusting the pork chops

2 tablespoons good-quality balsamic vinegar

1 cup seedless purple grapes

1 cup small grape tomatoes

¹/₄ cup sliced fresh basil leaves

▶ Prepare the Squash Puree as directed on page 105. Keep it hot until serving time.

▶ To start the fruit sauté, heat a large ovenproof skillet over medium heat. Add the grapeseed oil to coat the skillet. Add the leeks and apples, sauté until soft, but still holding their shape. Season to taste with salt and pepper. Transfer the sauté to a parchment-lined cookie sheet.

▶ Preheat the oven to 375°F.

▶ Using the same skillet, add some more grapeseed oil to coat the bottom. Heat until hot, but not smoking.

▶ In the meantime, pat the pork chops dry, and season with salt and pepper on both sides. Pour some flour onto a plate. Dredge the pork chops in the flour. Add the chops to the pan and cook for about 4 minutes without turning them; they should be golden brown on the bottom. Turn the chops with large tongs, and brown the other side for about 4 minutes. Immediately transfer the skillet to the oven and finish cooking the chops for about 7 minutes, or until pink in the center.

(continued)

- Transfer the pork chops to a plate, cover with aluminum foil and let them rest a few minutes.

- Place the leeks and apples back in the used skillet. Use more grapeseed oil if necessary. Add the vinegar and heat until warm. Add the grapes and tomatoes, and just warm them through. Season again with salt and pepper if needed.

- **To assemble:** Place ½ cup of the squash puree in the middle of each plate, top with a layer of the sautéed fruit mixture and drippings from the skillet, some sliced basil, a pork chop, and some more basil on top for garnish. Serve immediately.

SERVES 4

Squash Puree

Use this rich and colorful puree as a side dish, or as a bed for various meats or fish. Use whatever fresh herbs you have on hand, such as rosemary or thyme, to make it a savory puree. You could also add freshly grated nutmeg or ground cinnamon, and maple syrup to make it a sweet puree.

1 butternut squash (1½ pounds), peeled, seeded, and cut into chunks

1 teaspoon kosher salt

1 tablespoon finely chopped sage

2 tablespoons unsalted butter

2 tablespoons half-and-half

2 cups chicken broth or water

Freshly ground black pepper

▶ Put squash and salt in a large saucepan and cover with water or broth. Bring to a boil until it is fork tender, about 20 minutes. Pour off most of the water and return the squash to the saucepan. Add the sage, butter, and half-and-half. Puree with an immersion blender in the saucepan, or mash the squash until it is the desired consistency. Check for seasonings and add more salt and pepper to taste.

▶ Keep hot by transferring the puree to a glass mixing bowl, and placing it over the saucepan partially filled with simmering water.

SERVES 6

Elegant Apple Cake

My mother used to make this cake for company only. It is one of my childhood favorites. The cake is so moist and so easy that it can be made anytime, though for me it ushers in fall! Keep the pieces very small as the dessert is very rich.

Cake

1 cup vegetable oil

2 cups sugar

2 large eggs, at room temperature

1 teaspoon pure vanilla extract

2 cups flour

1½ teaspoons baking soda

1 teaspoon kosher salt

1 teaspoon ground cinnamon

3 cups chopped and peeled Granny Smith apples (4-6 apples)

½ cup chopped walnuts

Topping

½ cup sugar

½ teaspoon cinnamon

Sauce

1 stick (8 tablespoons) unsalted butter

1 cup sugar

½ cup cream

1½ teaspoons pure vanilla extract

¼ teaspoon freshly grated nutmeg

▶ Preheat the oven to 350°F. Butter and flour a 9x13-inch baking pan.

▶ **To make the cake:** In a large bowl, mix together the oil, sugar, eggs, and vanilla until combined. Sift together the flour, baking soda, salt, and cinnamon and add to the egg and sugar mixture. Blend until combined. Stir in the apples and nuts. Pour the batter into the prepared pan.

▶ In a small bowl, stir together the sugar and cinnamon for the topping. Sprinkle the topping over the cake batter, and let it sit for 1 hour. Bake for 1 hour or until a tester comes out clean. Let the cake cool.

▶ **To make the sauce:** Combine the butter, sugar, and cream in a medium saucepan over medium heat. Stir until the butter melts, and the mixture boils and begins to thicken. Watch carefully so the sauce doesn't burn on the bottom of the pan. Remove it from the stove and stir in the vanilla and nutmeg. Set aside to cool. Transfer the sauce to a small pitcher.

▶ To serve, cut the cake into squares. Pass the pitcher of sauce.

SERVES 12

This salmon dinner is a dazzler for family and friends. It is a very simple and healthy dinner, full of lots of fresh vegetables, texture, and color. Baking the salmon in aluminum foil keeps the fish very moist and flavorful. The julienned vegetables offer great texture and a beautiful presentation. Serve it in the foil or not, and put it in large wide soup bowls, just like they do in the fancy restaurants. Don't leave a drop of the delicious broth. And when was the last time you had a leafy spinach salad *not* made from the baby spinach variety? This salad will become part of your new salad repertoire and is a great source of calcium and iron.

Talk to the wine guy at your favorite shop about sparkling wine. You should be able to find a great bottle from the United States, Italy, Germany, Australia, or New Zealand for under $20 a bottle. The sparkling wine pairs well with the date appetizer. Use a Sauvignon Blanc for the fish broth, and finish the bottle with dinner. For those family members or guests who don't drink alcohol, offer something special such as club soda with pomegranate or freshly squeezed blood orange juice. The ratio should be about 3:1 club soda to fruit juice.

For an extra touch, serve the mini crisps on a paper-doily-lined dessert plate. If you have some mini cream pitchers, use them for each place setting. Your family and guests will think they are dining at a 3-star restaurant!

The Day Before

▶ **Wash and dry the spinach**
▶ **Wash the vegetables for the salmon bundles**

Salmon Soirée

Warm Dates with Goat Cheese

Sparkling Wine

▲ ▲ ▲

Spinach Salad with Mushrooms

▲ ▲ ▲

Roasted Salmon and
Vegetable Bundles

Non-Oakey Chardonnay
or Sauvignon Blanc

▲ ▲ ▲

Mini Cranberry-Apple Crisps

▲ ▲ ▲

Coffee

Warm Dates with Goat Cheese

This is a sweet and savory appetizer that is very versatile. For tasty variations, try using bacon or pancetta instead of prosciutto, walnuts instead of pistachios, and try pears instead of dates. If you can't find goat cheese, you could substitute feta cheese.

CONNIE'S NOTES: *For a restaurant touch, use an inexpensive squeeze bottle to drizzle the honey and balsamic vinegar over the dates.*

¼ cup goat cheese, at room temperature

1 tablespoon chopped pistachio nuts

2 tablespoons fresh thyme leaves

8 large dates, pitted

8 small slices prosciutto (about 2x2 inches)

Extra-virgin olive oil, honey, and good-quality balsamic vinegar for drizzling

Thyme sprigs, for garnish

Pistachio nuts, for garnish

▶ Preheat the oven to 425°F.

▶ In a small bowl, stir together the goat cheese, nuts, and thyme. Stuff the dates with the goat cheese mixture, and press the dates back together into one piece. Wrap a piece of prosciutto over each date and secure the prosciutto in place with a round toothpick. Place the dates in a small baking dish. Drizzle lightly with olive oil.

▶ Bake for about 15 minutes. Remove the dates from the oven and transfer to a serving plate. Drizzle lightly with honey and balsamic vinegar. Garnish with thyme sprigs, additional pistachios, and serve warm.

SERVES 4

Spinach Salad

This is a simple and unusual salad that is best made with whole spinach, not baby spinach (the texture and full flavor of the spinach is necessary for this salad). Be sure to wash the spinach and spin it dry—there's nothing worse than a gritty spinach salad! Check for tough stems and discard them.

Salad

One 10-ounce bag leafy spinach, washed and dried

$1/2$ medium red onion, sliced very thin

2 ounces blue cheese, crumbled

2 cups sliced white button mushrooms

Vinaigrette

1 clove garlic, finely minced

$3/4$ teaspoon kosher salt

$1/4$ teaspoon chopped fresh thyme leaves

2 tablespoons red wine vinegar

$1/4$ teaspoon freshly ground black pepper

1 teaspoon Dijon mustard

6 tablespoons extra-virgin olive oil

1 hard-boiled egg, for garnish

- Place the spinach, onion, and cheese in a large bowl.
- **To make the vinaigrette**: In a small bowl, whisk together all the ingredients except for the oil. Slowly drizzle in the olive oil until the dressing emulsifies.
- Place a very small amount of the dressing in a separate bowl with the mushrooms and toss gently. Add the mushroom mixture to the salad bowl; add the rest of the dressing just until the salad is lightly moistened. Serve the salad immediately family style or on individual plates, and top with some sliced egg.

SERVES 4–6

Roasted Salmon and Vegetable Bundles

Several years ago, we had an assembly line going in my kitchen on Valentine's Day. I was helping friends make the salmon recipe for their dates. At that time, we used parchment paper instead of aluminum foil. Unfortunately, the salmon took about an hour to cook in parchment paper. The timing of the dinner was thrown off, so we all kept drinking champagne. We have learned that foil works better than parchment paper. (And, two of the couples are now married!)

1 teaspoon thyme leaves

4 tablespoons unsalted butter, softened

2 leeks, white parts only, julienned

2 medium carrots, julienned

1 red pepper, julienned

4 tablespoons extra-virgin olive oil

Four 5-ounce fresh salmon fillets, about $1\frac{1}{2}$ inches thick, bones removed

Juice of 2 lemons

$\frac{1}{2}$ cup dry white wine

Kosher salt and freshly ground black pepper

12 sprigs thyme

Lemon wedges, for garnish

▶ Preheat the oven to 425°F. Cut four 16x16-inch squares of heavy-duty aluminum foil and set aside.

▶ Stir the thyme leaves into the butter.

▶ Place the julienned vegetables in a bowl. Place the foil pieces on the kitchen counter, and begin an assembly line. Place one-quarter of the vegetables on each foil piece, salt and pepper, drizzle with olive oil, and place a salmon fillet on top. Sprinkle with lemon juice, wine, salt and pepper, 2 thyme sprigs, and a tablespoon of thyme butter. Wrap tightly with the foil, and place on a cookie sheet.

▶ Bake for about 15 minutes, depending on your oven. When the salmon is done, transfer the contents of each bundle (including the juices) to a large shallow soup bowl. Drizzle with olive oil, garnish with a wedge of lemon and a thyme sprig, and serve immediately.

SERVES 4

CONNIE'S NOTES: *Leeks have been prized by gourmets for many years. They look like giant scallions and are related to the garlic and onion families, but their flavor is more subtle and the fragrance is milder than onions or garlic. Leeks can have lots of hidden dirt and sand between the multiple layers. Cut each leek in half and soak in water to remove the dirt before you slice them.*

The salmon can be prepared a couple of hours in advance and refrigerated. When you plan to roast the salmon, bring the packets to room temperature. Salmon is cooked when a fork flakes the salmon easily. The salmon packets could also be prepared on the top level of a medium-high grill. The flavor will be different than roasting the salmon in the oven.

With tweezers, be sure to check the salmon fillet for additional thin bones.

To **julienne** *(joo-lee-EHN)* is to cut food into very thin strips or matchsticks.

Mini Cranberry-Apple Crisps

Everyone loves apple crisp, but the cranberries make this dessert a little different. Keep the dessert small, and limit it to several bites, just like they do in Europe. Everyone will be satisfied, and not feel guilty. With proper planning, you should be able to eat the dessert warm, just like in your favorite restaurant. (Adapted from *Bon Appétit*)

CONNIE'S NOTES: *Use the slicing disc of your food processor or a mandoline to slice the apples. The job will be done uniformly and quickly.*

Topping

¹/₂ cup packed dark brown sugar

¹/₃ cup old-fashioned oatmeal

¹/₃ cup flour

2 teaspoons ground cinnamon

¹/₂ teaspoon freshly grated nutmeg

1 stick (¹/₂ cup) plus 2 tablespoons chilled unsalted butter, cut into pieces

¹/₂ cup pecan halves

Filling

2 pounds (4–6 medium) Granny Smith apples, peeled, cored, and cut into ¹/₂ inch-thick slices

³/₄ cup fresh cranberries, or use frozen cranberries that have been thawed

2 tablespoons sugar

1 teaspoon cinnamon

¹/₂ teaspoon freshly grated nutmeg

▶ Preheat the oven to 375°F. Butter 6–8 (3¹/₂-inch) mini soufflé dishes or small glass dishes. (Alternatively, use a square cake pan.) Place on a cookie sheet and set aside.

▶ **To make the topping:** Combine the brown sugar, oatmeal, flour, cinnamon, and nutmeg in a bowl. Add the ¹/₂ cup butter and using your hands or a knife, cut it in until small pieces form. Add the pecans and mix by hand.

▶ For the filing, combine the apples, cranberries, sugar, cinnamon, and nutmeg in a bowl and toss gently. Divide the apple mixture among the soufflé dishes. Top with the oatmeal mixture, and dot with the remaining 2 tablespoons butter. Bake uncovered for about 45 minutes. If you overbake these crisps, they will turn into mushy applesauce.

▶ Serve plain, with heavy cream, or with a scoop of ice cream.

SERVES 6-8

If you can't go to Barcelona, why not re-create it at home? Traveling to Barcelona, in my opinion, means: bright colors, fabulous shoes, Gaudí architecture, tapas, tomatoes, saffron, pork, manchego cheese, almonds, garlic, rioja, paprika, sherry, and lots of fresh seafood I've never seen before. What is most noticeable in all the small restaurants are tapas, or small plates. I've tried to incorporate the colors and flavors of Barcelona in this menu that includes several tapas served with cava, and a main course of smoky pork tenderloin. The meal is topped off with some berries and chocolate, and don't forget the strong coffee. Spaniards love their coffee and drink it all day long. At home, they spice it with cinnamon and lots of sugar.

Serve the mussels in a large bowl and let your family help themselves. How about using those brightly colored plastic buckets you might use at the beach for the shells? Keep some crusty country bread nearby to sop up the flavorful broth from the mussels.

The wines in this menu deserve special mention. Serve cava (CAW-va) with the tapas, just like they do in Barcelona. Cava is an inexpensive Spanish white or rosé sparkling wine. It is less sweet than champagne, and about half the price. You should be able to find cava in a wine shop or your wine merchant can order it for you. See how you think it compares to champagne. In tapas restaurants, many times cava and other wines are served in a regular water glass, nothing fancy here. Rioja (ree-O-ha) is a spicy red Spanish wine from the northern part of Spain. It is supposed to be the best wine in the world in terms of value for your money. It is mostly made from tempranillo grapes. Rioja will stand up well to the spicy pork tenderloin and beans.

Salud!

The Day Before

▶ **Roast the peppers**

▶ **Chop the vegetables for mussels**

▶ **Prepare the pork**

A Night in Barcelona

Roasted Red Peppers with Manchego Cheese and Serrano Ham

Spicy Mussels
Crusty Country Bread
Cava

Pork Tenderloin with White Beans and Spinach
Rioja

Fresh Fruit with Chocolate Sauce

Espresso

Roasted Red Peppers with Manchego Cheese and Serrano Ham

I first made this recipe in a cooking/art week in Provence. Sarah Brown, the home chef and art historian, showed us how to make this very simple recipe. (For more information on this program, go to www.week-in-provence.com.) If you want to serve the peppers as small tapas, use small pieces of pepper, or one-half of each roasted pepper.

6 large sweet red peppers, halved and seeded

Extra-virgin olive oil

1/2 pound aged manchego cheese, thinly sliced

1/2 pound thinly sliced Serrano ham

2 tablespoons finely minced flat-leaf parsley

▶ Preheat the oven to 425°F.

▶ Place the peppers in a bowl and drizzle with olive oil. Place the peppers skin side up on a cookie sheet lined with parchment paper. Roast until the skins are blackened and blistered, about 30 minutes. Remove from the oven and let cool. Carefully remove the skin from the peppers and discard it. (Don't rinse the peppers as you will rinse away the flavor.)

▶ To assemble, lay each pepper on a flat surface, top with a slice of cheese, then a slice of ham. Roll up, and transfer to a plate. Top with the parsley and drizzle with olive oil. Serve at room temperature on a serving platter.

SERVES 4–6

CONNIE'S NOTES: *Manchego (mahn-CHAY-goh) is Spain's most famous cheese. It is a golden, semi-firm sheep's milk cheese that has a full mellow flavor. You should be able to find this delicious cheese in a specialty food store or cheese shop. A good substitution would be any firm sheep's milk cheese, Monterey Jack, or white cheddar.*

I wouldn't recommend jarred roasted peppers for this recipe. They tend to have a bitter aftertaste.

Serrano *(se-RAW-noh)* ham is a country ham from Spain that is cured for a year. It has a deeper flavor and firmer texture than the Italian prosciutto.

Spicy Mussels

Restaurant food made easily at home! This recipe can be varied a lot of ways. Simply change the spices, add Pernod or pastis (French liqueurs), or add some cream. This dish could also make a quick dinner by increasing the amount of mussels per serving and adding a salad.

CONNIE'S NOTES: *Mussels are very inexpensive and easy to make at home. You can find live mussels at your fish market, or in two-pound mesh bags at the grocery store in the fish department for about $4.00. If any of the mussels have opened, do not buy them, and throw them away if you find them at home. Put the mussels on ice in the refrigerator, and use them the same day.*

Most mussels are debearded now, but if they are not, remove the attached black piece that looks like a sliver of steel wool. Give the beard a tug, pull it off, and discard. Rinse the mussels before you plan to use them.

2 tablespoons extra-virgin olive oil

1 rib celery, finely chopped

2 cloves garlic, finely chopped

1 small onion, finely chopped

1 medium carrot, peeled and diced

2 fresh bay leaves

4 sprigs thyme

1 teaspoon kosher salt

1/4 teaspoon freshly ground black pepper

2 Roma tomatoes, chopped

2 teaspoons sweet Spanish paprika

2–3 cups dry white wine

2 pounds live mussels, scrubbed and debearded

1 tablespoon finely chopped flat-leaf parsley, for garnish

Small loaf of crusty white bread for dipping

▶ In a Dutch oven, heat the olive oil over medium heat. Then add all the ingredients except for the wine, mussels, and parsley. Sauté until the vegetables are soft, about 15 minutes. Add the wine, and deglaze the pan, scraping down the bits on the bottom of the pan. Cover and simmer for about 15 minutes. Add more wine, if it has cooked down too far.

▶ Add the mussels, cover, and simmer for about 2 minutes, or until all the mussels open. Serve immediately with bread for dipping and extra bowls for the empty shells.

SERVES 4

Pork Tenderloin with White Beans and Spinach

This recipe seems complicated, but it's not. It really is a meal in itself with protein, vegetables, and great color.

CONNIE'S NOTES: *To clean the coffee grinder after pulverizing the chiles, pulverize some soft bread. It will remove most of the residue from the chiles. Discard the bread afterwards.*

Truffle oil can be found in 3-ounce bottles in specialty stores. It is expensive, so use it sparingly. A little truffle oil goes a long way, but it will be the "wow" in this recipe!

Dry Rub
6 dried ancho chiles

6 dried chipotle chiles

2 tablespoons mustard seed

$\frac{1}{2}$ teaspoon kosher salt

$\frac{1}{2}$ teaspoon freshly ground black pepper

Beans
$\frac{1}{4}$ pound slab bacon, diced

2 cloves garlic, minced

1 tablespoon thyme leaves

2 cups (16 ounces) dried Great Northern beans

1 teaspoon kosher salt

Pork
2 tablespoons canola oil

2 pork tenderloins, about 1 pound each

$1\frac{1}{2}$ cups chicken or beef stock

2 tablespoons unsalted butter

Two 9-ounce bags baby spinach, washed

White truffle oil, for drizzling

Kosher salt and freshly ground black pepper

Thyme sprigs for garnish

▶ **The day before:** Preheat the oven or toaster oven to 350°F. Roast the chilies for 10 minutes on a cookie sheet. Remove from the oven, and cool. Grind the chilies and mustard seed into a fine powder with a mortar and pestle or a coffee grinder. Rub the pork with salt and pepper, and then coat with the chili mixture. Cover with plastic wrap and refrigerate overnight.

▶ **To prepare the beans:** The day of serving, in a soup pot, render the bacon over medium heat for about 10 minutes. Add the garlic and sauté another minute. Add the thyme, beans, and salt. Cover the beans with water and simmer for about an hour, or until the beans are tender, but not mushy. Check for seasonings.

▶ Preheat the oven to 500°F.

(continued)

- Preheat a skillet large enough to hold the tenderloins and stock. When the skillet is hot, add enough canola oil to coat the bottom. Sauté the tenderloins on both sides until they have a nice dark brown color, about 3 minutes per side. Add the stock and transfer the skillet to the oven.

- Roast the pork for 5 minutes for medium-rare. Remove the skillet from the oven, take out the tenderloins and let them rest for several minutes before slicing. Cover them with foil to keep them warm.

- Place the skillet with the stock back on the stove, and reduce by half. Add the butter to the stock, then add the spinach and cook until its wilted.

- **To serve:** Place some beans in the center of each serving plate, mound some of the spinach on top of the beans. Top with several slices of pork, and some of the juice from the spinach. Drizzle with truffle oil, garnish with thyme sprigs, and serve.

SERVES 4

Fresh Fruit with Chocolate Sauce

I was first given this chocolate sauce as a Christmas gift from my flutist friend, Lydia. It is so easy and so good that you will use it over fruit, on pound cake, as chocolate fondue, and wherever else you like chocolate.

Sauce

One 12-ounce can evaporated milk

2 cups sugar

1/4 teaspoon kosher salt

4 ounces good-quality unsweetened chocolate, finely chopped

1 teaspoon pure vanilla extract

Fruit

2 cups seasonal fruit: strawberries raspberries, blueberries, blackberries, or fresh pineapple chunks

▶ **To make the sauce:** In a heavy saucepan, combine the evaporated milk, sugar, and salt. Stir until combined. Bring the mixture to a rolling boil, and boil for 2 minutes. Remove from the stove, add the chocolate, and stir until melted. Stir in the vanilla. Store covered in the refrigerator. Before using, microwave at 50 percent power for 30 seconds.

▶ **To serve:** Just before you plan to eat the berries, carefully wash them, sort for moldy or hard ones, and drain the excess water. Place them on a paper towel to dry. Put a combination of berries or pineapple in a martini glass or wine glass. Drizzle with the warm chocolate sauce and serve.

SERVES 4; MAKES ABOUT 2 CUPS SAUCE

This is one of those menus for after a long hard day— who says you can't have eggs for supper? Slip into something comfy, put on your slippers, turn on a soothing CD, and light your favorite candle. Relax with the family in front of the fireplace and eat dinner served family style on the coffee table. Start with the bean dip and offer some crunchy crudités. Then enjoy this light and cheesy soufflé with a French-inspired butter lettuce salad. This meal is so simple and so good you may never eat scrambled eggs again!

Start the soufflé, and bake it. Toss the salad, and prepare the dressing. While the soufflé is baking, serve the beets and olives. Perhaps this is an unusual appetizer combination you've not tried before. The earthiness of the beets balances the saltiness of the olives very well. Serve the beets with small plates and forks. To increase everyone's comfort, put out some simple cotton placemats on the coffee table, and eat there. Serve the salad and soufflé together. Remember the soufflé will deflate quickly so eat it right when it comes out of the oven. Eating at the coffee table may become a regular event, sort of like a picnic inside for the whole family.

Finish the supper with some homemade biscotti and freshly brewed herbal tea. Put loose tea leaves or tea bags in your favorite teapot, and pour over boiling water. Top the teapot with a tea cozy, and give it several minutes to brew properly. Serve with honey and lemon.

The Day Before

▶ **Roast the beets**

▶ **Make the biscotti**

▶ **Make the dip**

▶ **Wash the lettuce and prepare crudités**

Thursday Night Supper

Mas's White Bean Dip with Crudités

Roasted Beets with Olives

Gruyère and Parmesan Soufflé

Butter Lettuce Salad

White Rhône

Anise, Pine Nut, and Golden Currant Biscotti

Freshly Brewed Tea

Mas's White Bean Dip

Here's a nice spicy white bean dip that's a little different from the norm. (Adapted from Mas Restaurant in Chicago's Bucktown neighborhood)

CONNIE'S NOTES: *This recipe is better if it is made ahead of time. I don't recommend using canned beans for this recipe. The flavor is much better by cooking the dried beans. For an added touch, pile the dip in a green or red pepper that has been seeded (cut a thin slice off the bottom of the pepper so it will stand up).*

Chipotles (*chih-Poht-lays*) in adobo sauce are very spicy so a little goes a long way. You can buy the chipotles in 4-ounce cans. Store the remaining chipotles in a covered container in the refrigerator, they will keep for several months.

1 cup dried white beans, such as Great Northern or cannellini

1/4 pound slab bacon or 4 slices thick-cut bacon, diced

1 clove garlic, crushed

2 sprigs fresh thyme

1 tablespoon ground cumin

1 tablespoon hot chili powder

1 tablespoon minced chipotle chilies in adobo sauce

3–4 tablespoons extra-virgin olive oil

1 teaspoon kosher salt

1/4 teaspoon freshly ground black pepper

Thyme sprigs, for garnish

▶ Wash the beans in a colander, discarding any shriveled ones. Cook the bacon over medium heat in a large stockpot until it is cooked but not crisp. Add the garlic, and cook 1 minute. Add the beans, thyme, and enough water to cover by at least 3 inches. Bring to a boil. Reduce the heat, and simmer, partially covered, until the beans are tender, skimming off foam that rises. This process will take about 1½ hours.

▶ Drain the beans and bacon and remove the thyme sprigs. Transfer the bean mixture to a food processor. Add the cumin, chili powder, chipotles, and ½ teaspoon of the salt. Process for about 1 minute. Slowly add the olive oil, and blend until a chunky texture is achieved. Taste, add any additional salt that is needed, and mix in the black pepper.

▶ Transfer the dip to a covered plastic container and refrigerate. When you are ready to serve the dip, bring it to room temperature. Garnish with thyme sprigs and serve with assorted crudités (such as endive, pepper spears, broccoli and cauliflower florets, carrot sticks, and those cherry tomatoes in a mesh bag that taste pretty good in the wintertime) and crackers.

SERVES 8–10

Roasted Beets with Olives

A nice unusual appetizer or salad, this recipe could also be used as a quick brown-bag lunch with a slice of Italian bread.

CONNIE'S NOTES: *Roast the beets in advance, and use them in this appetizer and in green salads. Roasted beets keep well in the refrigerator.*

1 pound medium-size beets, red and golden, washed and cut in half

2 teaspoons plus 1 tablespoon extra-virgin olive oil

1/2 teaspoon kosher salt

1/4 teaspoon freshly ground black pepper

1/4 cup good-quality black olives, drained

Zest of 1 lemon

1 tablespoon minced Italian parsley

Parsley sprigs, for garnish

▶ Preheat the oven to 400°F. Line a cookie sheet with parchment paper.

▶ Place the beets cut side down on the cookie sheet. Drizzle 2 teaspoons of the olive oil over them, and sprinkle with the salt and pepper. Roast for about 45 minutes, or until fork tender. Remove the beets from the oven, and let cool before removing the skins.

▶ Cut the beets into wedges. Place them in a small bowl, add the olives, lemon zest, parsley, and a turn of freshly ground black pepper. Drizzle with 1 tablespoon olive oil, stir, and serve. Garnish with several parsley sprigs and serve with small plates and forks.

SERVES 4

Gruyère and Parmesan Soufflé

Great any night, this fluffy, cheesy dish makes a perfect light dinner. My husband will not eat scrambled eggs for dinner but he will eat this soufflé. It may appear difficult, but it isn't if you follow all the steps. The soufflé is a "wow" when you take it out of the oven, but it will deflate quickly.

CONNIE'S NOTES: *Make sure the bowl for the egg whites is very clean and oil free. Otherwise the egg whites will not reach their proper volume.*

Experiment using different herbs in this savory soufflé, such as fresh thyme, herbes de Provence, and fresh sage.

To keep track of when you bought the eggs, mark the date on the box when you come home from the grocery store.

½ stick (4 tablespoons) unsalted butter

5 tablespoons flour

Pinch of cayenne pepper

1 teaspoon kosher salt

¼ teaspoon freshly ground black pepper

Pinch of freshly grated nutmeg

1¼ cups whole milk

¼ cup dry white wine

1½ tablespoons sliced fresh tarragon leaves

1 cup grated Gruyère cheese (about 4 ounces)

½ cup plus 4 tablespoons freshly grated Parmesan cheese, for topping

6 extra-large egg yolks, at room temperature

8 extra-large egg whites, at room temperature

▶ Position a rack in the center of the oven and preheat to 400°F. Generously butter a 5-cup soufflé dish. Sprinkle with 2 tablespoons of the Parmesan cheese and set aside.

▶ Melt the ½ cup butter over medium heat in a medium saucepan. Add the flour, cayenne, salt, pepper, and nutmeg. Cook until brown, and the mixture starts to bubble, whisking constantly. Add the milk and wine slowly, and continue to whisk until the mixture is thick, about 2 minutes. Remove from the stove, stir in the tarragon, the Gruyère and the ½ cup Parmesan cheese. Let the sauce sit until it is at room temperature (the cheese does not have to be melted).

▶ While the sauce is cooling, whisk the egg yolks until foamy. Beat the egg whites separately until they hold soft peaks, but are not dry. Pour the egg yolks into the cooled sauce, and stir, Lighten the sauce with a little bit of the beaten egg whites, and fold in gently. Fold the rest of the egg whites into the sauce.

▶ Transfer the mixture to the soufflé dish, top with the remaining 2 tablespoons of Parmesan cheese, and place in the oven. Immediately turn the oven down to 375°, and bake until the soufflé is golden and puffed, about 45 minutes. Serve immediately.

SERVES 4

Butter Lettuce Salad

A favorite in French bistros, this salad is delicate, crisp, delicious, and looks beautiful anytime. It reminds me of a house salad in France.

CONNIE'S NOTES: *Butter lettuce is also known as Boston or Bibb lettuce. It is available all year round.*

Have you every wondered why vinaigrettes made with Dijon mustard in France taste different than they do in the United States? When Dijon mustard is shipped to the United States, more sugar is added for this marketplace. If you take a trip to France, purchase some inexpensive Dijon mustard in the local grocery store, or go directly to the Maille mustard store in Paris.

Walnut oil is readily available in many grocery stores now, and is lighter tasting than olive oil. This light vinaigrette matches very well with the buttery lettuce leaves.

2 small heads butter lettuce, washed and dried

1 carrot, shredded

6 cherry tomatoes, halved

Vinaigrette
1 tablespoon Dijon mustard

1/2 teaspoon kosher salt

1/4 teaspoon freshly ground black pepper

1/2 teaspoon fresh thyme leaves

2 tablespoons fresh lemon juice

1/4 cup walnut oil

▸ Break the lettuce heads into leaves and place them in a medium salad bowl. Top with the carrot and tomatoes.

▸ In a small bowl, whisk together the mustard, salt, pepper, thyme, and lemon juice. Slowly add the oil, and whisk together until it emulsifies. Toss the amount of dressing you want with the salad, and serve immediately.

SERVES 4

Anise, Pine Nut, and Golden Currant Biscotti

The best homemade biscotti I have tasted! Biscotti *(bee-SKAWT -tee)* is a twice-baked Italian cookie. This recipe was given to me by Tara Lane, a pastry chef in Chicago. She makes 400 biscotti a week, but this recipe has been revised for the home chef. Try using other ingredients that you like in biscotti such as dried cranberries and cherries, chocolate chunks, walnuts, etc. My favorite way to eat biscotti is to dunk them in espresso.

CONNIE'S NOTES: *Wrap several biscotti in cellophane bags, and give as a homemade gift, wrapped in the colors of Italy of course.*

2 sticks (1 cup) unsalted butter, at room temperature

1¹/2 cups sugar

4 large eggs, at room temperature

4 cups flour

¹/2 teaspoon kosher salt

1 cup pine nuts

Zest of 1 orange

Zest of ¹/2 lemon

¹/2 teaspoon anise seeds

1¹/2 cups golden currants

1 egg, beaten for glazing

Raw sugar crystals

▶ Cream together the butter and sugar until fluffy. Add the eggs, one at a time, until the mixture is thick and lemon colored. Stir in the flour and salt. Mix until combined. Stir in the pine nuts, zest, anise seeds, and currants.

▶ Divide the dough into three pieces. Lightly flour a pastry board, and roll each piece of dough into a log, about 2 inches wide and 12 inches long. Work quickly as the dough is sticky. Instead of placing more flour on your fingers, put a small amount of cold water on your hands. Don't overwork the dough. Place the logs on a cookie sheet lined with parchment paper and refrigerate for about an hour.

▶ Preheat the oven to 325°F.

▶ Glaze the chilled biscotti logs on the top and sides with the beaten egg. Sprinkle raw sugar all over the biscotti. Bake for about 45–50 minutes, or until golden brown. Remove from the oven, and cool completely.

▶ Reduce the oven temperature to 300°F. Using a serrated knife, cut the biscotti into slices on an angle, about ¹/2 inch thick. Place the biscotti on a parchment-lined baking sheet, and bake again until golden brown, or about 20 minutes. Cool completely, and then store in sealed plastic containers. The biscotti should keep for about a week.

MAKES 4–5 DOZEN

This meal reminds me of many Sunday suppers we had as children in rural Kansas. My mother would always make a pot of soup, and my four siblings and I would make some homemade dessert to practice our culinary, reading, and math skills. This menu is a 21st-century version of one of those 1960 suppers of soup and salad, but it lets you take advantage of all the new produce and pantry items that are readily available today. The meal begins with a roasted garlic and sun-dried tomato appetizer, then moves on to creamy pumpkin soup that's been updated with cardamom and served with a hearty salad of cannellini beans, tuna, and greens. For a retro finish there are old-fashioned brownies and milk.

Eat this meal at the counter and enjoy it in stages. Serve the soup and salad family style, and let everyone help themselves. (It's the weekend and Mom is supposed to be off.)

Viognier is a full-bodied white wine that is a nice complement to this menu. Viognier wines were first barreled in Condrieu, France, but California vineyards are making this wine a fast-rising star. It was on the brink of extinction in the 1960s, but has made a comeback. You will notice the distinctive aroma of fruits and flowers of the wine, but it will be dry on the palate. It will pair nicely with the salad and soup. The price per bottle is all over the board so ask your favorite wine person about the wine before you buy anything over $20 per bottle.

Why not take out the red-and-white checked napkins and placemats and brighten your table during the doldrums of winter? Pour the glasses of milk, and pull out the Scrabble or Monopoly games. Enjoy a cozy night in!

The Day Before

▸ **Make the soup**

▸ **Prepare the salad greens**

Soup's On

Garlic and Sun-Dried Tomato Dip with Italian Bread

Rosé

▪ ▪ ▪

Spicy Pumpkin Soup

Green Salad with Cannellini Beans and Tuna

Viognier

▪ ▪ ▪

Buttermilk Chocolate Brownies

Milk

Garlic and Sun-Dried Tomato Dip

This is my niece's favorite because she loves roasted garlic and tomatoes together.
(Adapted from *Bon Appétit*)

CONNIE'S NOTES: *Once I attempted to save time by trying to roast garlic in the microwave. This does not work! The kitchen was very smoky and the garlic was black and burnt. Garlic needs to be kept moist, tightly covered, and cooked in a medium-hot oven.*

If you are using sun-dried tomatoes that are not in olive oil, soak them in olive oil to reconstitute them. This reconstitution should take about an hour, or until they are soft.

Herbes de Provence (*EHRB duh proh-VAWNS*) is an assortment of dried herbs that are commonly used in southern France. Some common herbs in the mixture are: rosemary, sage, summer savory, marjoram, fennel seed, lavender, basil, and thyme. If you don't have herbes de Provence, just use the dried herbs that you have on hand.

2 large heads garlic, unpeeled

2–3 tablespoons extra-virgin olive oil

2–2¹/₂ cups chicken broth

1 cup sun-dried tomatoes in oil, chopped

2 teaspoons herbes de Provence

Freshly ground black pepper

4–6 ounces plain goat cheese, sliced

1 cup loosely packed fresh basil leaves, cut into slivers (chiffonade)

Basil sprigs, for garnish

Small loaf of Italian bread or mini toasts

▶ Preheat the oven to 350°F.

▶ Slice a small amount off the top of the garlic heads, and remove any loose outer white papery skin. Place the garlic in a medium casserole dish. Drizzle the garlic with the olive oil, chicken broth, tomatoes, herbs, and pepper to taste. Tightly cover with aluminum foil and bake until tender, about 1¹/₂ hours.

▶ Remove from the oven and arrange the goat cheese around garlic. Bake, uncovered, for about 10 minutes, or until the cheese is melted. Top with basil chiffonade, and garnish with basil sprigs. To serve, squeeze the roasted garlic out of each clove onto a piece of bread or mini toast and top it with some of the tomato, basil, and cheese mixture.

SERVES 6–8

Spicy Pumpkin Soup

A delicious soup with some hidden kicks! Try to use that sugar pumpkin from Halloween, or any other left-over pumpkins to make this flavorful easy soup. This soup requires no cream for its silkiness. An immersion blender works very well for this recipe and guarantees no mess! Take the leftovers in a brown-bag lunch the next day.

CONNIE'S NOTES: *If you wear contact lenses or rub your eyes frequently, you may want to wear gloves when you are seeding or chopping hot peppers.*

8 cups peeled sugar pumpkin (2 medium or 1 large) cut into 1-inch chunks

1/4 cup grapeseed oil

1 yellow onion, coarsely chopped

8 cloves garlic, minced

1 teaspoon kosher salt

1/2 teaspoon freshly ground black pepper

1 teaspoon sugar

1 teaspoon ground cardamom

4 cinnamon sticks

1/2 jalapeño pepper, seeded and chopped

1 cup apple cider

6 cups chicken stock, preferably homemade

▶ Preheat the oven to 350°F.

▶ In a large mixing bowl, mix together the pumpkin, grapeseed oil, onion, garlic, salt, and pepper. Spread the mixture on a large baking sheet lined with parchment paper. Roast for approximately 30 minutes or until the pumpkin is fork tender.

▶ Transfer the pumpkin mixture to a large soup pot. Add the remaining ingredients, and cook, covered, over medium heat until the pumpkin is very tender and mushy, about 45 minutes. Discard the cinnamon sticks or use for a potpourri on the stove. Leave the soup in the pot and puree it with an immersion blender until smooth. Taste for seasonings, and adjust consistency to your taste by adding more chicken stock if needed.

▶ Serve hot, with a dollop of sour cream if desired, and a sprinkling of cinnamon or toasted pumpkin seeds.

SERVES 4 AS AN ENTRÉE, 6–8 AS A STARTER COURSE

Green Salad with Cannellini Beans and Tuna

Cannellini beans make this salad substantial enough for an entrée. This is a very quick salad to prepare and would also be wonderful for lunch with a cup of soup.

CONNIE'S NOTES: *Italian tuna is very flavorful, meaty, and rich and tastes very different from the tuna we usually use for tuna sandwiches. It can be found in some grocery stores in the Italian section, or at Italian specialty stores, and online. Try this tuna and you will find out how tasty canned tuna can be.*

Mesclun (MEHS-kluhn) is a mixture of young, small salad greens that can be found in many supermarkets. It is also called salad mix or gourmet salad mix. Commonly included greens are: arugula, frisée, oak leaf, mache, radicchio, and sorrel.

Arugula (ah-ROO-guh-la) is a bitterish, aromatic salad green with a peppery mustard flavor.

Radicchio (rah-DEE-kee-oh) is a red-leafed Italian chicory that is most often used as a salad green. It has a slightly bitter taste and is most often seen in the U.S. looking like a red and white tiny cabbage.

2 cups mixed fresh lettuces or mesclun greens

One 3.2-ounce can Italian tuna in oil, drained

3 ounces ($1/2$ cup) baby arugula

1 endive, thinly sliced

8 cherry tomatoes, halved or quartered, depending on size

$1/2$ cup thinly sliced radicchio

$1/2$ cup thinly sliced red onion

$1/4$ cup flat-leaf parsley leaves

1 tablespoon fresh oregano leaves, lightly chopped

Kosher salt and freshly ground black pepper

2–4 tablespoons extra-virgin olive oil

2 tablespoons good-quality balsamic vinegar

One 14-ounce can cannellini beans, rinsed and drained

▶ Arrange the lettuces, tuna, arugula, endive, tomatoes, radicchio, onion, parsley, and oregano on a medium platter or in a shallow, medium-sized salad bowl. Sprinkle with salt and pepper, and drizzle lightly with the olive oil and vinegar. Place the beans in the middle of the salad, sprinkle the beans with additional salt and pepper, and serve immediately.

SERVES 2–4 AS AN ENTRÉE, 6–8 AS PART OF AN ANTIPASTI PLATTER

Buttermilk Chocolate Brownies

Here's another one of my mother's favorites—easy and moist cakelike brownies in under an hour! This recipe has been in our family for at least 25 years. If you need a dessert for a bake sale or a work function, these are the brownies to make.

Brownies

1 stick (8 tablespoons) unsalted butter

¼ cup good-quality unsweetened cocoa powder, such as Droste

1 cup water

½ cup vegetable oil

2 cups flour

2 cups sugar

½ teaspoon kosher salt

1 teaspoon baking soda

½ cup buttermilk

2 eggs, beaten at room temperature

1 teaspoon good-quality pure vanilla extract

½ cup toasted pecans, chopped (optional)

Frosting

1 stick (8 tablespoons) unsalted butter

¼ cup good-quality unsweetened cocoa powder

⅓ cup buttermilk

1 teaspoon pure vanilla extract

16 ounces confectioners' sugar

▶ Preheat the oven to 375°F. Grease and flour a 12x17-inch sheet pan. Shake off the excess flour.

▶ **To make the brownies:** Combine the butter, cocoa, water, and vegetable oil in a small saucepan, and bring to a boil. Remove it from the stove. Sift the flour, sugar, salt, and baking soda into a large bowl. Pour the cocoa mixture over the dry ingredients. Do not stir. Immediately add the eggs and vanilla and mix until smooth. The batter will be runny.

▶ Pour into the prepared pan and bake for approximately 15–20 minutes or until a toothpick comes out clean. While the brownies are baking, make the frosting.

▶ **To make the frosting:** In the same small saucepan that you used for the brownies, combine the butter, cocoa, buttermilk, and vanilla, and stir. Bring to a boil. Remove from the stove, add the confectioners' sugar, and stir together until blended and smooth. When you take the brownies out of the oven pour the frosting over them right away and spread it to the edges. Top with the pecans. When the brownies are set and cooled, cut them into squares.

MAKES 16–20 BROWNIES

Who doesn't love an Italian meal from start to finish? This menu is designed for those of us who love Italian food but are tired of the traditional spaghetti with tomato sauce. Instead, this meal starts with all your favorite antipasti, and glides into the main course of polenta and sausages spiced and sweetened with flavorful balsamic vinegar and red grapes. There's plenty of Chianti to wash down the Italian flavors. And for the grand finale there's an authentic Italian dessert—hazelnut cake served with a sparkling dessert wine.

Do you have any red or green placemats left over from the Christmas holidays? Alternate them on your table, and pair them with white napkins to complete the Italian color scheme. Use some bunches of fresh herbs, such as sage, rosemary, and thyme, and place them in a simple vase instead of flowers. Your table will smell good too.

Serve an inexpensive Chianti with the main meal, and espresso or Moscati with the dessert. Moscati is a sweet, semi-sparkling white wine from the Piedmont region of Italy. It is low in alcohol, inexpensive, and high in sugar. The *Wine Enthusiast* says, "There are wines that you drink for sheer pleasure, here and now, with no strings attached." Moscati D'Asti is one of those wines. In Italy, they drink their cappuccinos before noon, and espressos later in the day. I once made the mistake of ordering cappuccino with dinner in Rome (like Americans do). Everyone in the restaurant stared at me.

The Day Before

▶ **Make the cake**

Italian Night

Antipasti Platter

Italian Bread

Chianti

▲ ▲ ▲

Sausage and Grape Sauté on Polenta

More Chianti

▲ ▲ ▲

Hazelnut-Almond Cake

▲ ▲ ▲

Espresso

Moscati d'Asti

Antipasti Platter

Antipasto (*ahn-tee-PAHS-toh*) means "before the meal." This Italian term refers to hot or cold hors d'oeuvres. If it is summertime, use fresh tomatoes and melon. The Italians like to spend time coordinating the colors of the antipasti platter, sort of like doing a puzzle. Have fun with it!

CONNIE'S NOTES: *Many of the antipasti suggestions here can be found at your local grocery store in the deli or ethnic foods sections. If you have an Italian deli in your neighborhood or town, by all means make a visit. The person behind the counter will be happy to recommend his or her favorites for an antipasti platter.*

Italian olives (such as Liguria, Gaeta, and Lugano)

Large caper berries

Thinly sliced prosciutto

Roasted red and yellow peppers (recipe below)

Chunks of Parmigiano-Reggiano

Pepperoncini

Giardiniera (mixed pickled vegetables found in a jar)

Small buffalo mozzarella balls

Cherry tomatoes and fresh basil

Sliced smoked meats such as bresaola (dried beef tenderloin), salami, cappocolo, abbruze, soppressata, or genoa

Extra-virgin olive oil

White anchovies

Grilled eggplant

Marinated mushrooms

Kosher salt

Freshly ground black pepper

Loaf of Italian bread

▶ Select 4–6 of the items above for the antipasti platter and arrange on a large platter with small plates and forks for self service.

Roasted Peppers

▶ Preheat the oven to 425°F.

▶ Cut red and yellow peppers in half and remove the seeds, stem, and white pith. Place the peppers (skin side up) on a cookie sheet lined with parchment paper. Drizzle with olive oil. Roast for 15–20 minutes, or until the skins turn black. Remove the peppers from the oven and let cool.

▶ When the peppers are cool to the touch, pull off the skins and throw them away. Do not rinse the peppers as you will rinse away flavor. Place the peppers in a plastic container and refrigerate. When you are ready to use them, bring the peppers to room temperature.

Sausage and Grape Sauté on Polenta

One of the great Italian comfort meals, this is a "stick-to-your-bones" dish best served in the cooler months. If you can find fresh Italian sausages at your Italian deli, buy them. You will appreciate the fresh homemade taste. The grapes add just a bit of sweetness to the dish, and another texture to the plate. The Fontina cheese and milk add a creamy texture to the polenta. The Parmesan cheese adds a nice bite.

CONNIE'S NOTES: *Polenta is finely ground cornmeal from Italy. It can be found in the Italian section of your grocery store in a small bag or small plastic container.*

1 tablespoon extra-virgin olive oil

4 sweet or hot Italian sausages

$1/2$ cup balsamic vinegar

1 tablespoon unsalted butter

$3/4$ cup red grapes, halved and seeded

$1^1/2$ cups chicken broth, preferably homemade

$1^1/2$ cups whole milk

1 tablespoon chopped fresh thyme or rosemary

2 cloves garlic, minced

1 teaspoon kosher salt

1 cup coarse polenta

$3/4$ cup grated Fontina cheese (about 3 ounces)

$1/2$ cup freshly grated Parmesan cheese (about 2 ounces)

▶ Coat the bottom of a medium skillet with the olive oil, and heat over medium heat. When the pan is hot, add the sausages and brown on both sides. Add the balsamic vinegar, butter, and grapes. Cover, and simmer over low heat for about 10 minutes while you make the polenta.

▶ In a medium saucepan, simmer the broth, milk, thyme, garlic, and salt over low heat for 20 minutes. Gradually whisk in the polenta. Cook and stir until the polenta is thick and creamy, about 5 minutes. Add the cheeses and stir until they are melted.

▶ Divide the polenta among four plates. Top with one sausage, and some of the grapes and drippings from the skillet. Garnish with sprigs of thyme or rosemary and serve.

SERVES 4

Hazelnut-Almond Cake

This is a delicious, not-too-sweet way to complete an Italian meal. It is a dense cake that should be served in small slices. (Adapted from *Cucina* magazine)

CONNIE'S NOTES: *The original recipe called for hazelnut paste, which is not readily available to home chefs. The almond paste is available in the baking section of your grocery store in cans and plastic packages. Almond paste is a mixture of blanched ground almonds, sugar and glycerin. It is less sweet than marzipan and slightly coarser. It should be firm but pliable. Leftover almond paste can be tightly covered and stored in the refrigerator.*

1 cup hazelnuts, toasted for about 5 minutes, and cooled (save several for garnish)

1¼ cups flour, plus more for pan

10 tablespoons unsalted butter, at room temperature

¾ cup sugar

¼ cup almond paste, at room temperature

3 eggs, at room temperature

2 teaspoons almond extract

½ teaspoon kosher salt

1 teaspoon baking powder

Good-quality unsweetened cocoa powder, for dusting

⬧ Preheat the oven to 325°F. Prepare an 8-inch round cake pan by spreading about 2 teaspoons of vegetable oil over the bottom of the pan. Scatter flour all over the pan, and shake off the excess.

⬧ Rub off the skins of the hazelnuts. Place the nuts and ¼ cup of the flour in the bowl of a food processor. Pulse until the nuts are finely ground.

⬧ In the bowl of an electric mixer, cream together the butter and sugar until very light. Beat in the almond paste. Add the eggs one at a time, and beat after each addition. Scrape down the bowl with a rubber scraper, add the almond extract, and combine.

⬧ In a small bowl, mix together the nuts and the remaining 1 cup flour, salt, and baking powder. Add the dry ingredient mixture to the batter, and mix until just combined. The batter may look curdled, but that's fine. Pour the batter into the prepared pan.

⬧ Bake for 25–30 minutes in the center of the oven. The cake is done when the cake tester comes out clean. Allow the cake to cool in the pan for 10 minutes, and then gently transfer it to a simple cake plate. When cool, sift cocoa powder over the top, and decorate the center with several whole hazelnuts.

SERVES 10–12

Do your sports events start with chips, dip, and take-out pizza in a cardboard box? This menu is a lot more fun, with hearty appetizers of sausage and cheese kabobs and lighter tomato/basil/mozzarella kabobs. The home run is a tasty chili made with beans, ground turkey, and lots of vegetables, but don't tell anyone. The meal is finished with your choice: crisp apples or gooey caramel corn. Of course, no party is complete without lots of ice-cold beer and apple cider for the youngsters. This is a casual meal that could be served for any sports event, like a Super Bowl, Final Four, a World Series game, or a televised debate.

Let your family and guests help themselves all evening while they eagerly watch the live action on TV. Reheat the chili in the slow cooker so it stays hot. Find crisp apples, such as Honey Crisps, and serve them in a rustic bowl or one of your modern silver pedestal bowls. Give guests their own small brown bags of caramel corn tied with raffia. Serve the beer on ice in the kitchen sink, just like in college. Put the hot apple cider in a coffee thermos, and let people pour their own into a coffee mug. Garnish the cider with cinnamon sticks and orange slices.

Hollow out a pumpkin and fill it with a bunch of fragrant eucalyptus for the buffet table. Start your own pot of potpourri by placing lemon slices, orange slices, cinnamon sticks, bay leaves, cardamom and fennel seeds, and whole cloves in a medium saucepan. Cover with water, and let it simmer on the stove and fill your house with the smells of upcoming holidays.

Pull out those Halloween and fall placemats, and use coordinating dish towels to keep the décor very casual. Set up the buffet table on the kitchen counter, and roll up the placemats and napkins and place them in a wicker basket or an old metal bucket. You might even want to think about using some high-quality disposable tableware so everyone can enjoy the game.

The Day Before

▸ **Make the caramel corn**

▸ **Make the chili and cook overnight**

World Series Party

Mozzarella, Tomato, and
Basil Kabobs

Salami, Provolone, and
Pepperoncini Kabobs

▪ ▪ ▪

Turkey Chili

Tortilla Chips

▪ ▪ ▪

Mom's Caramel Corn

Bowl of Apples

▪ ▪ ▪

Dark Beer and
Hot Apple Cider

Mozzarella, Tomato, and Basil Kabobs

This appetizer will remind you of summer. Try to find the mesh bags of tomatoes in the wintertime.

8 ounces small, fresh mozzarella balls, drained

12 medium basil leaves

12 small cherry tomatoes

Round 3¹/₂-inch toothpicks or 4-inch bamboo forks

Kosher salt and freshly ground black pepper

Extra-virgin olive oil

Basil sprigs, for garnish

▶ **To assemble:** Alternate a mozzarella ball, basil leaf, and tomato on each toothpick. Arrange the kabobs on a plate, and drizzle olive oil all over them. Sprinkle with kosher salt and freshly ground cracked black pepper. Garnish with small sprigs of basil and serve.

SERVES 4–6

Salami, Provolone, and Pepperoncini Kabobs

A twist on the typical ham and cheese spread, the pepperoncini adds a nice kick.

CONNIE'S NOTES: *You can find the round toothpicks or bamboo forks in the baking aisle.*

Pepperoncini *(pep-per-awn-CHEE-nee)* is an Italian pickled pepper readily found in most grocery stores or Italian markets. Sometimes they can be quite spicy. To serve these kabobs, you might want to stick them into miniature pumpkins and place on a tray.

¹/₂ pound chunk of salami, cut into 1-inch cubes

¹/₂ pound chunk of Provolone cheese, cut into 1-inch cubes

12 pepperoncini, drained and stemmed

Round toothpicks or 4-inch bamboo forks

▶ **To assemble:** Alternate the salami, provolone, and peppers on each toothpick.

SERVES 4–6

Turkey Chili

The ingredient list looks like everything but the kitchen sink, but it is very easy to make. This is a very thick and chunky chili. The cinnamon adds that hidden "wow" that tastes similar to Cincinnati chili. It's a great way to get out your slow cooker for fall meals.

CONNIE'S NOTES: *If you like the chili thinner, add some warmed vegetable or chicken broth.*

Cannellini beans are medium-sized ivory kidney beans that are very popular in Tuscany. They have a nutty flavor and smooth texture and absorb the flavors of strong herbs. They can be found both dried and canned.

One 15-ounce can black beans, drained and rinsed

One 15-ounce can kidney beans, drained and rinsed

One 15-ounce can red beans, drained and rinsed

One 15-ounce can light kidney beans, drained and rinsed

One 15-ounce can cannellini beans, drained and rinsed

One 28-ounce can crushed tomatoes

One 12-ounce bottle dark beer

2 tablespoons olive oil

1 large onion, chopped

3 cloves garlic, finely chopped

2 stalks celery, chopped

1/2 red pepper, seeded and diced

1/2 yellow pepper, seeded and diced

2 carrots, diced

1 jalapeño pepper, seeded and finely chopped

2 pounds ground dark turkey meat

1 1/4 teaspoons cinnamon

1 1/2 teaspoons kosher salt

1 teaspoon cumin

1 teaspoon freshly ground black pepper

1 teaspoon Spanish paprika

1 1/2 teaspoons chili powder

▶ Place all the beans, the tomatoes, and beer in a six-quart slow cooker. Set on high. Heat the olive oil in a large skillet, and sauté all the vegetables over medium heat until the vegetables are soft. Remove the vegetables from the skillet and put them into the slow cooker.

▶ Add the turkey to the used skillet, break into chunks, and brown over medium heat until it is cooked through. Add all the spices to the browned meat, and sauté together for about 15 minutes over medium heat. Add this mixture to the slow cooker, and leave on high for 2 hours.

▶ Check seasonings, and turn the slow cooker to the low setting for 4 hours. Serve with your favorite tortilla chips.

SERVES 6–8

Mom's Caramel Corn

This tasty caramel corn rivals the famous Garrett's popcorn in Chicago! My mother used to give this out to trick-or-treaters in our small Kansas town. Place the popcorn in airtight plastic bags, and then put it in small colored gift bags tied with pipe cleaners. It makes a great gift for the holidays.

CONNIE'S NOTES: *If you leave out the oven step, the popcorn will be very very hard!*

Popcorn
$^1/_2$ cup vegetable oil

1 cup popcorn

Caramel
2 cups dark brown sugar

2 sticks (16 tablespoons) unsalted butter

$^1/_2$ teaspoon salt

$^1/_2$ cup white corn syrup

$^1/_2$ teaspoon baking soda

2 teaspoons pure vanilla extract

1 cup unsalted peanuts (optional)

▶ **To prepare the popcorn:** Add the oil to a large heavy pan. Heat the oil over medium heat, and add several kernels of popcorn. When you hear and see it pop, add the popcorn and cover the pan. When it finishes popping, remove from the stove and pour onto a paper towel. Let it cool, and pick out the unpopped kernels. Transfer the popcorn to a large bowl. You will have approximately 8 cups of popped corn.

▶ Preheat the oven to 250°F. Line several baking sheets with parchment paper.

▶ In a medium heavy saucepan, stir together the brown sugar, butter, salt and corn syrup. Bring to a rolling boil over medium heat, and boil for exactly 5 minutes, stirring occasionally. Turn off the stove and add the baking soda and vanilla. Stir, and pour the caramel over the popcorn. Add the peanuts. Stir the mixture quickly, and pour onto the baking sheets. Flatten the mixture out.

▶ Bake for 1 hour, remove from the oven, and let it cool. Store the caramel corn in a tightly covered container.

SERVES 8–10

Here is an elegant dinner for one of those wintry nights at home for just you and your significant other, *after* the kids have gone to bed. It starts with some bubbly champagne and warmed almonds and moves on to melt-in-your-mouth lamb chops served on top of roasted root vegetables and topped with a red wine sauce. Celebrate the meal, and the evening, with a creamy panna cotta sweetened with honey.

Pull out a white damask tablecloth and the matching napkins. Use your fine china and stemware that you use only once a year. Buy a bunch of red roses and place them in one of your beautiful vases. You'll feel like you've been transported to some fancy restaurant, while being in the comfort of your own home. Turn on the fireplace, light the candles, and enjoy the food and solitude.

Oftentimes, you can find half bottles of champagne at your wine store. If not, they can order a half bottle for you. Then you won't waste any of the champagne. Enjoy the unusual wintry salad right before the main course. Don't forget to use some of the burgundy in the wine sauce, and enjoy the rest with the lamb. Finish off the meal with a bit of chocolate, just like the French do. (This menu may become your special occasion once a year.)

Cheers!

The Day Before

▸ **Prepare the almonds**

▸ **Make the panna cotta**

▸ **Roast the beets**

▸ **Make the rub for lamb**

▸ **Cut the vegetables for roasting and cover with water**

Romantic Dinner for Two

Toasted Almonds with Rosemary

Half-Bottle Champagne

◗ ◗ ◗

Roasted Beet Salad with
Shaved Fennel, Watercress, and
Crème Frâiche Dressing

◗ ◗ ◗

Rack of Lamb with
Rosemary and Wine Sauce

Roasted Root Vegetables

Red Burgundy

◗ ◗ ◗

Panna Cotta

Chocolate-Covered Cherries

◗ ◗ ◗

Coffee

Toasted Almonds with Rosemary

Toasting almonds intensifies their flavor and adds crunch. You'll want to keep these on hand for a snack for the next sports event or for a movie at home. They are especially good warmed just before serving. Serve in individual ramekins and garnish with a sprig of rosemary, and feel like you are flying first class.

1½ cups unsalted almonds

1 tablespoon minced fresh rosemary

1 tablespoon sea salt

2 tablespoons vegetable oil

▶ Preheat the oven to 350°F.

▶ Place all the ingredients on a 12x18-inch cookie sheet, combine with your hands, and spread out the nuts to cover the cookie sheet. Bake for approximately 20 minutes. Remove from the oven, cool, and put in a tightly covered container.

SERVES 2

Roasted Beet Salad with Shaved Fennel, Watercress, and Crème Fraîche Dressing

This salad is a takeoff on one served at the Lake Park Bistro in Milwaukee. It has unusual flavors, is light, and looks as good as it tastes.

CONNIE'S NOTES: *This salad could also be served as a main-course lunch for one person if you doubled the ingredients.*

Crème fraîche is a mature thickened cream that has a slightly tangy flavor, and a velvety texture. It can be found in the cheese section of your grocery store in small 4-ounce containers. Sour cream could be used as a substitute. You can make crème fraîche at home by mixing together 1 cup whipping cream and 2 tablespoons buttermilk in a glass container. Cover and let it stand at room temperature for at least 8 hours or until thickened. Stir well, cover, and refrigerate for up to 10 days. You can use crème fraîche on top of warm cobblers, and in spreads and dips.

1 medium red beet

Kosher salt

Freshly ground black peeper

1 tablespoon extra-virgin olive oil

1/2 small fennel bulb, thinly sliced

1 small bunch watercress, tough stems removed

1/4 small red onion, thinly sliced

Dressing

1/4 cup crème fraîche

1/4 teaspoon kosher salt

1/8 teaspoon freshly ground black pepper

1/2 teaspoon grated horseradish

1 tablespoon fresh lemon juice

▶ **To roast the beet:** Preheat a small oven to 400°F. Wash the beet and cut in half lengthwise. Place it cut side down on a piece of aluminum foil on a small cookie sheet. Sprinkle with the salt, pepper, and extra-virgin olive oil. Roast for about 35 minutes or until tender. Remove from the oven and cool. Remove the skin and cut into 1/2-inch slices. (You might want to roast more beets and refrigerate them for later use.)

▶ Arrange the beet slices in an overlapping circle on a plate.

▶ Combine the fennel, watercress, and onion in a bowl. Mix together the dressing ingredients. Toss with the vegetable mixture. Check the seasonings.

▶ Spoon the vegetable mixture on top of the beet slices, making sure the beets still show on the plate. Serve immediately.

SERVES 2

Rack of Lamb with Rosemary and Wine Sauce

This is so easy and foolproof that you may never order rack of lamb in a fancy restaurant again! Buy the best quality lamb that you can find. Ask your butcher to trim it for you. Serve the lamb chops on top of Roasted Root Vegetables (the next recipe).

CONNIE'S NOTES: *It is important to not overcook the lamb. Don't go past medium rare or the lamb will be tough. It should be so tender that it will melt in your mouth. You could also grill the rack of lamb and eliminate the wine sauce.*

Lamb

¹/4 cup plus 2 tablespoons extra-virgin olive oil

2 tablespoons Dijon mustard

2 cloves garlic, minced

1 teaspoon chopped fresh rosemary leaves

¹/4 teaspoon freshly ground black pepper

One ³/4 pound rack of lamb

Rosemary sprigs, for garnish

Sauce

¹/2 shallot, thinly sliced

¹/2 cup red wine

1–2 tablespoons beef stock

1 tablespoon unsalted butter

Salt and pepper

▶ **To prepare the lamb:** Form a paste with ¹/4 cup of the olive oil, mustard, garlic, rosemary, and pepper. Spread it over the rack of lamb, covering both sides. Let sit at room temperature for about one hour. (While the lamb is marinating, prepare the Roasted Root Vegetables as directed in the next recipe. Cover with foil to keep warm.)

▶ Preheat the oven to 400°F.

▶ Heat an ovenproof skillet and add the remaining 2 tablespoons olive oil. When the pan is very hot, sear the lamb chops on both sides until golden brown. Immediately transfer the pan to the oven, and roast for about 10 minutes for medium-rare, or to 130°F on a meat thermometer.

▶ Remove the skillet from the oven, and transfer the lamb to a platter (don't wash the skillet, you make the sauce in it), and let it rest for at least 10 minutes before carving into individual chops. (While the lamb is resting you can reheat the root vegetables in the oven if desired.)

▶ **To make the sauce:** Sauté the shallot in the used skillet until tender. Add the wine and deglaze the pan by scraping the bits off the bottom of the pan. Bring to a boil, reduce by half, add the beef stock, and bring to a boil again. Remove from the stove, add the butter, and stir until melted. Taste for seasonings.

▶ To serve, place the roasted vegetables on the bottom of a serving plate, and place the lamb chops on top. Drizzle the wine sauce over the lamb and vegetables, garnish with sprigs of rosemary, and serve.

SERVES 2 GENEROUSLY, OR ABOUT 3 SMALL LAMB CHOPS PER PERSON

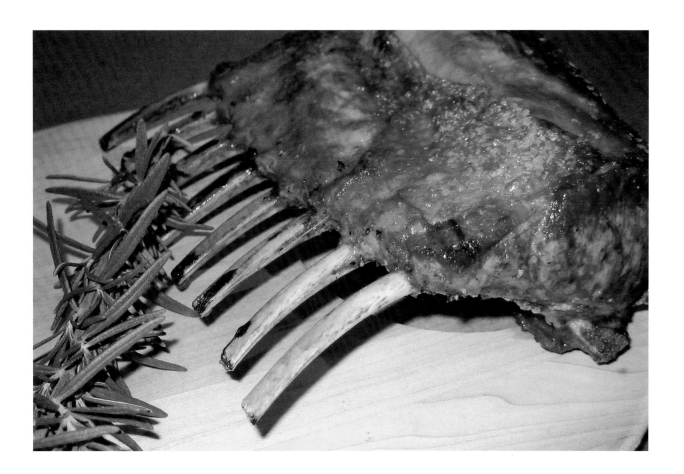

Roasted Root Vegetables

The vegetables caramelize in the oven and the flavors combine to make a great side dish, which could be served with pork, beef, or chicken. This recipe makes a lot more than needed for your dinner for two, but the leftovers make a great vegetarian lunch or an accompaniment to a dinner of grilled chicken and brown rice.

CONNIE'S NOTES: *Experiment using your favorite root vegetables, such as unusual squashes or yams, and other fresh herbs like savory or thyme. If you want a lighter flavor, substitute grapeseed oil for the olive oil.*

Make sure the vegetables are cut into similar size chunks so they cook evenly. To save time, the vegetables can be prepped the day before by placing them in a large bowl, and covering them with water. Place them in a covered container in the refrigerator. Drain them, and then proceed with the rest of the directions.

1 medium sweet potato, peeled and cut into 1-inch chunks

1 medium leek, white part only, sliced

$1/2$ medium red onion, peeled and cut into $1/4$-inch chunks

1 medium turnip, peeled and cut into 1-inch chunks

1 parsnip, peeled and cut into 1-inch chunks

2 large carrots, peeled and cut into 1-inch chunks

1 small butternut squash (about 1 pound), peeled and cut into 1-inch chunks

1 small pumpkin (about 1 pound), peeled, and cut into 1-inch chunks

1 small acorn squash, (about 1 pound), peeled and cut into 1-inch chunks

1 medium baking potato, peeled and cut into 1-inch chunks

2 tablespoons chopped fresh sage

$1/2$ tablespoon kosher salt

$1/2$ teaspoon freshly ground black pepper

2 tablespoons extra-virgin olive oil

▶ Preheat the oven to 425°F. Line a cookie sheet with parchment.

▶ In a large bowl, mix all the ingredients together (using 1 tablespoon of the sage), and spread out on the cookie sheet. Roast for about 25 minutes, or until the vegetables are fork tender. Remove from the oven and cool slightly. Check for seasonings and add the remaining tablespoon of sage. Serve on a platter.

SERVES 6

Panna Cotta

Panna cotta (*PAHN-nah-KOH-tah*) is a light, silky Italian pudding/custard that is made without eggs. It can be either savory or sweet. One vegetarian restaurant in Chicago serves an avocado panna cotta which is delicious. This recipe is for dessert. Feel free to experiment with the base of this recipe, and add new ingredients.

CONNIE'S NOTES: *This is the best panna cotta I have found, not too soft, and not too hard in texture. It has the consistency of crème brûlée. The granulated gelatin works very well and is readily available. Panna cotta would also be very good for a hot summer dessert served with seasonal fresh berries.*

*It's very important **not** to boil the milk because the milk and cream will curdle and become unusable. Other than that, the dessert is very simple and is a winner.*

1½ cups heavy cream

1½ cups whole milk

¼ cup honey

1 vanilla bean, scraped

One package (¼ ounce) unflavored gelatin

2 tablespoons cold water

1 teaspoon pure vanilla extract

1 cup berries, if available

2 tablespoons confectioners' sugar

6 mint leaves for garnish

▶ Combine the cream, milk, and honey in a medium saucepan, and stir. Add the vanilla bean and scrapings, and bring to a low simmer. While the milk is simmering, dissolve the gelatin in the water in a small dish. Let it set for about 10 minutes.

▶ Remove the saucepan from the stove, add the gelatin mixture and vanilla extract to the hot milk, and stir until dissolved. Remove the vanilla bean.

▶ Oil six 3½-inch ramekins lightly with salad oil. Pour the milk and cream mixture into the ramekins, and refrigerate for at least 6 hours. The panna cotta will become firm, but will jiggle slightly in the ramekin.

▶ When ready to serve, remove two the ramekins from the refrigerator. Run a knife around the edges, and invert onto dessert plates. Garnish with berries, confectioners' sugar and mint leaves. Serve right away. Keep any extra servings in the refrigerator, and eat them tomorrow.

SERVES 6

Chocolate-Covered Cherries

This recipe offers a little different twist on the usual chocolate-covered strawberries. Be sure to leave the cherry stem on for easy dipping and presentation. These will keep for about a day at room temperature.

CONNIE'S NOTES: *Strawberries can be substituted for the cherries if there are no fresh cherries. Use whatever fruit tastes the best and is in season. If you're serving guests, make a few extra, and send home the extras in a small cellophane bag tied with raffia. By using good-quality bittersweet chocolate, your craving for chocolate will be satisfied with one or two bites.*

4 ounces good quality bittersweet chocolate, 70 percent cocoa

8 cherries with stems

▶ Melt the chocolate in small bowl over simmering water, or a double boiler. Dip each cherry in the chocolate, leaving the top of the cherry uncovered. Place the cherries on a piece of waxed paper. Dry for several hours.

SERVES 2

Are you in the mood for old-fashioned comfort food? Does the thought of tasty, moist meat loaf, green beans with bacon, and cheesy scalloped potatoes make your mouth water? Is pineapple upside-down cake one of the favorite desserts from your youth? Then this menu is for you. It originated about 10 years in Chicago in my high-rise apartment. Somehow, the word got around that we were having meat loaf and people started inviting themselves over. It became Meat Loaf Moments because of all of the fond memories surrounding the food from our childhood.

Don't forget to put out any gingham placemats and napkins that you might use for a summer picnic. It's comfort food and it's cold outside, so keep it cheery and homey. Start your meal with one of your favorite amber beers, and then add a hearty red wine with the meat loaf.

When was the last time you used your deviled egg plate? Pull it out and use it. Update the classic carrot gelatin salad by putting the salad squares in martini glasses and garnishing each with lettuce, and place in front of each place setting. Serve the rest of the meal family style. Put the green beans and sliced meat loaf on the same plate. Pass the scalloped potatoes. Grind some fresh coffee beans, add some filtered water, and end the meal with delicious cup of coffee to go with the pineapple cake. Enjoy!

The Day Before

▶ **Make the gelatin salad**

▶ **Boil the eggs**

▶ **Prepare the meat loaf to the baking stage**

Deviled Eggs

Stuffed Celery Sticks

Amber Beer

● ● ●

My Favorite Meat Loaf

Scalloped Potatoes

Fresh Green Beans with Bacon

Carrot-Pineapple Gelatin Salad

Chianti

● ● ●

Pineapple Upside-Down Cake

● ● ●

Coffee

Deviled Eggs

Good anytime!

4 small eggs

1 teaspoon kosher salt

Filling
¼ teaspoon salt

¼ teaspoon freshly ground black pepper

¼ teaspoon dry mustard

1 tablespoon grated onion

½ tablespoon sour cream

1 tablespoon mayonnaise

Garnish
1 tablespoon chopped red bell pepper

1 tablespoon chopped green pepper

⅛ teaspoon paprika

▶ Carefully place the eggs in a medium saucepan. Cover with cold water and add the salt. Bring the eggs to a boil quickly, uncovered. Cover the pan, remove from the stove, and let the eggs finish cooking for approximately 22 minutes. Immediately place the eggs in an ice-water bath to stop the cooking process.

▶ When the eggs are cool, peel them and separate the yolks from the whites. The yolks should be a bright lemon color, not have a greenish cast, which happens when they are overcooked.

▶ Finely chop the egg yolks and combine in a bowl with the filling ingredients. Mix until just combined. Mound the yolk mixture into the egg white halves. Garnish with the chopped peppers, and sprinkle with paprika. Refrigerate the eggs until you are ready serve.

SERVES 4–6

Stuffed Celery Sticks

A twist on a classic, these make a great after-school snack too!

¹/₄ cup chunky peanut butter

¹/₂ tablespoon soy sauce

2 tablespoons reduced-fat cream cheese, at room temperature

¹/₂ teaspoon grated orange zest

6 stalks celery, cut into 3-inch sticks

▶ Combine the peanut butter, soy sauce, cream cheese, and orange zest and stuff the celery sticks with it. Arrange pinwheel style on a small serving platter.

SERVES 4–6

My Favorite Meat Loaf

No one will believe it has carrots in it—they keep the meat loaf very moist. The leftovers are great for sandwiches.

CONNIE'S NOTES: *Be sure not to overwork the mixture. Use your hands to mix the meat loaf ingredients.*

2 tablespoons olive oil

1 medium yellow or white onion, diced

1/2 medium green pepper, diced

1/2 medium red pepper, diced

3 medium carrots, shredded

1 clove garlic, finely chopped

1 1/2 pounds ground chuck

1/2 pound ground pork

1 1/4 teaspoons kosher salt

3/4 teaspoon freshly ground black pepper

2 eggs, beaten

1/2 cup bread crumbs

1 tablespoon 2% milk

1/4 teaspoon red pepper flakes

1/2 cup barbeque sauce

1 tablespoon Worcestershire sauce

Sauce
1/2 cup catsup

1 tablespoon brown sugar

▶ Preheat the oven to 350°F.

▶ Heat the olive oil in a large skillet over medium heat. Add the onions, peppers, carrots, garlic, and 1/4 teaspoon each of salt and pepper. Sauté until the vegetables are tender and translucent, about 1 minute. Cool to room temperature.

▶ In a large bowl, combine the ground meats and the cooled vegetables. Add the eggs, bread crumbs, milk, pepper flakes, 1 teaspoon salt, 1/2 teaspoon pepper, barbecue sauce, and Worcestershire. Mix together with clean hands. Place in an 8x11-inch loaf pan.

▶ Stir together the catsup and brown sugar, and spoon it over the meat loaf. Cover with aluminum foil.

▶ Bake for approximately 50 minutes or until the juices run clear. Let the meat loaf rest for 5 minutes, and then slice and serve.

SERVES 8–10

Scalloped Potatoes

Here's a classic cheesy potato favorite that used to be a standard on potluck tables. These potatoes are particularly good with meat loaf and roast beef. For a restaurant touch, you could bake the potatoes in individual buttered ramekins.

CONNIE'S NOTES: *Don't use low-fat cheese as it won't melt properly.*

Red potatoes bake quicker than Yukon Gold potatoes in this recipe.

¹/₂ stick (4 tablespoons) unsalted butter

¹/₄ cup flour

2 cups whole milk

¹/₂ teaspoon salt

¹/₄ teaspoon freshly ground black pepper

Pinch of freshly grated nutmeg

¹/₂ cup plus 2 tablespoons grated mild cheddar cheese

7 medium red potatoes (2 pounds) thinly sliced and peeled

1 tablespoon grated onion

▶ In a medium saucepan, melt the butter over low heat; add the flour, stir, and cook until thickened, or 2 minutes. Add the milk and stir continuously over medium heat until the mixture is thick and smooth. Add the salt, pepper, nutmeg, and ¹/₂ cup of the cheese, stirring until the cheese has melted. Remove the pan from the heat.

▶ Preheat the oven to 350°F.

▶ Layer the potatoes and onion in a 6-cup covered casserole dish; salt and pepper each layer. Pour the cheese sauce over the potatoes.

▶ Cover and bake for approximately 45 minutes or until the potatoes are fork tender. Remove the cover, and sprinkle the remaining 2 tablespoons cheese on the potatoes. Bake, uncovered, until the cheese is melted and browned, approximately 3 minutes. Serve immediately.

SERVES 4–6

Fresh Green Beans with Bacon

Fresh beans are a must with this recipe—they need to be crisp, tender, bright green, and not mushy. This tasty side dish can also be served with roast chicken or turkey.

3 strips bacon, coarsely chopped

1 shallot, thinly sliced

1 teaspoon kosher salt

1 pound fresh green beans

Freshly ground black pepper

Juice of ½ lemon

▶ In a medium skillet, sauté the bacon until just crisp. Add the shallot and sauté for 2 more minutes. Set aside.

▶ In a large saucepan, bring 6 cups of water and the salt to a boil. Add the beans and boil for 3 minutes. Drain the water off, and immediately place the beans in an ice-water bath to stop the cooking process, and to keep the vibrant green color.

▶ Add the beans to the skillet with the bacon, and sauté together for several minutes until the beans are cooked through. Add pepper to taste and salt (if necessary).

▶ Just before serving, squeeze the lemon juice on the beans to enhance their freshness.

SERVES 4–6

Carrot-Pineapple Gelatin Salad

Freshly squeezed orange juice and freshly grated carrots make all the difference in this recipe!

One 10-ounce can pineapple tidbits

1 package orange-flavored gelatin

1 cup boiling water

⅓ cup finely chopped celery

1 cup coarsely shredded carrots (1½ medium fresh carrots)

⅓ cup freshly squeezed orange juice

Lettuce for garnish

▶ Drain the pineapple well, reserving ½ cup of the juice.

▶ Empty the gelatin into a large bowl. Add the boiling water, and stir thoroughly. Add the pineapple, celery, carrots, and orange and pineapple juices and stir. Place in individual molds or in a square 4-cup baking dish. Refrigerate for several hours until firm or overnight.

▶ Unmold the individual molds or cut the gelatin into large squares. Serve in martini glasses garnished with lettuce.

SERVES 4–6

Pineapple Upside-Down Cake

A 1950s favorite, you can even buy a molded skillet for this cake at kitchen stores. Did you know that home economics students in Dublin are still learning to make this cake?

CONNIE'S NOTES: *If the cake begins to brown too quickly, cover it loosely with aluminum foil.*

$^1/_3$ **cup unsalted butter**

$^2/_3$ **cup firmly packed light brown sugar**

1 cup flour

1 teaspoon baking powder

$^1/_2$ **teaspoon salt**

3 extra-large eggs, separated

1 cup sugar

$^1/_2$ **teaspoon pure vanilla extract**

One 20-ounce can pineapple slices, drained, reserve 5 tablespoons juice

Maraschino cherries, for garnish

2 tablespoons rum

Whipped cream

▶ Preheat the oven to 350°F.

▶ Melt the butter in a 9-inch cast-iron skillet, or another similar-sized baking dish. Add the brown sugar and stir well. Set the mixture aside, off the stove.

▶ Sift together the flour, baking powder, and salt in a bowl. Set aside.

▶ Beat the egg yolks at medium speed until they are thick and lemon colored. Gradually add the sugar and vanilla, continuing to beat. Add the dry ingredients to the yolk mixture, and stir in the reserved pineapple juice. Mix until combined.

▶ Beat the egg whites until stiff peaks form and hold their shape. Fold the whites into the cake batter. Put the pineapple slices on top of the brown sugar mixture in a single layer in the skillet. Pour the batter over the pineapple slices.

▶ Bake for 35–40 minutes. Don't overbake. When you take the cake out of the oven, immediately run a knife around the edges to begin loosening the cake from the pan. Cool the cake in the skillet for 30 minutes.

▶ To serve, invert the cake onto a serving plate. Place a maraschino cherry in the center of each pineapple ring. Lightly poke holes all over the cake with a fork. Drizzle rum over the cake. Cut into thin slices, and serve with a dollop of whipped cream. Sift confectioners' sugar over the cake if desired.

SERVES 6–8

You probably have had fondue before, but maybe not raclette cheese melted with a raclette maker. A raclette dinner is a fun and simple way for a group of six to celebrate the first snowfall of the season. The word raclette *(rah-KLEHT)* is derived from the French verb *racler* (to scrape). The star of the meal is raclette cheese which is a pungent cheese from France or Switzerland. I prefer the French version as it has more bite than its Swiss cousin.

With all the cheese, potatoes, and ham, a raclette dinner is a definitely a "stick to your bones" menu, so I've kept the appetizer light and the dessert simple.

Following the tapenade appetizer, you can serve the meal family style by starting with the salad, and then serving the raclette and accompaniments. The raclette maker is in the center of the table so you might want to keep flowers to a minimum. Perhaps individual bud vases with a brightly colored zinnia at each place setting would be nice touch. To complement the tapenade, try a non-oaked Chardonnay or a versatile Pinot Noir for the adults. For the kids, serve club soda with maraschino cherries, or Shirley Temples. Don't forget the bendable straws.

Why not bake the cookies when you are preparing the coffee and hot chocolate? The sinful cookies will be gooey and taste great with the beverages. Encourage everyone to take a walk afterwards and celebrate winter!

The Day Before

▶ **Make the tapenade**

▶ **Boil the eggs**

▶ **Make the cookie dough**

▶ **Wash the lettuce**

Raclette Repast

Black Olive Tapenade with
Baguette Slices and Quail Eggs

Champagne and Shirley Temples

▲ ▲ ▲

Mesclun Salad with
Cranberries and Pecans

Raclette with Cornichons
and Pickled Onions

Sliced Black Forest Ham

Boiled New Potatoes

Chardonnay or Pinot Noir

▲ ▲ ▲

Triple-Chocolate Chip Cookies

Coffee

Hot Chocolate with Marshmallows

Black Olive Tapenade

If you travel to the Provence region of France, you will be served this delicious tapenade (*TA-puh-nahd*)—a thick paste used as a condiment. Sometimes chefs in Provence chop the ingredients by hand, but I prefer the food processor. Any leftover tapenade is delicious with grilled swordfish or tuna.

CONNIE'S NOTES: *In Limoges, France, if your French baguette has a lot of holes, it is rumored to have been made by a baker who didn't tell the truth. This rumor might create some great dinner gossip!*

Kalamata (kaw-la-ma-ta) olives are dark-colored Greek olives. They are easily found in grocery stores. They often come in a jar, with or without pits.

Store the tapenade in a tightly covered container and it should keep for a week in the refrigerator. If the olive oil separates from the tapenade, just mix it again when it is at room temperature.

3 cloves garlic

1 cup pitted kalamata olives, drained

2 anchovy fillets

1 tablespoon drained capers

1 teaspoon fresh thyme leaves

1 teaspoon fresh rosemary leaves

1 tablespoon fresh lemon juice

2–3 tablespoons extra-virgin olive oil

Freshly ground black pepper

1 baguette, cut into 1/2-inch-thick slices

6 quail eggs

Thyme or rosemary sprigs, for garnish

▶ **To make the tapenade:** Finely chop 2 cloves of the garlic in a food processor. Add the olives, anchovies, capers, thyme, and rosemary and process until still chunky. Add the lemon juice. With the machine running, gradually add the olive oil, and process until it is all combined, but still a bit chunky. Transfer to a small dish, and add pepper to taste.

▶ **To boil quail eggs:** In a saucepan, cover the eggs with cold water and bring to a boil. Cook for about 11 minutes. Quail eggs can be purchased at specialty stores or special-ordered. If you can't find them, just use small eggs.

▶ **To prepare baguette slices:** Preheat the oven to 400°F. Arrange the baguette slices on a baking sheet. Bake until lightly browned and crisp, about 10 minutes. As soon as the bread slices are cool, take a cut piece of garlic and rub it over each bread slice.

▶ Serve the tapenade at room temperature with baguette slices and the quail eggs, sliced in half lengthwise. Garnish with sprigs of thyme or rosemary.

SERVES 6–8

Mesclun Salad with Cranberries and Pecans

A great fall and winter salad—the cranberries get very plump when they are softened, the endive and pecans add the crunch, the radicchio the color, and the parsley the fresh flavor. Because of the freshness of the salad, you may want to serve this salad at a holiday gathering too.

6 cups mesclun, washed and dried

2 endives, thinly sliced

1/2 cup parsley sprigs

1/4 head radicchio, thinly sliced

1/2 cup dried cranberries

Juice of 1 orange

1/2 cup toasted broken pecans

Dressing

Zest of 1 orange

1 teaspoon Dijon mustard

Leftover orange juice from the drained cranberries

1/2 teaspoon kosher salt

1/4 teaspoon freshly ground black pepper

1 tablespoon honey

1/4 cup grapeseed oil

▶ Toss together the mesclun, endive, parsley, and radicchio. Refrigerate until ready to serve.

▶ Soften the dried cranberries in the orange juice for at least 1 hour, or until they plump up. Just before adding the cranberries to the salad, drain the juice and use it in the dressing.

▶ Whisk together all the dressing ingredients. Pour just enough dressing over the greens to lightly coat them. At the last minute, add the pecans to the salad and toss. Serve the salad family style.

SERVES 6

Raclette with Cornichons and Pickled Onions

Raclette is prepared with a raclette maker that melts the cheese over an electric burner that usually holds six individual cheese trays and paddles to scrape the cheese from the rind. You put the melted cheese on top of potatoes that have been smashed on your plate, then add the ham, pickles, and onions. You and your family can have fun enjoying this Swiss tradition.

CONNIE'S NOTES: *To purchase a raclette maker, visit the internet and type in key word "raclette." Also, raclette makers can be purchased at Roberts European Imports (800-968-2517) in the small Swiss town of New Glarus, Wisconsin. Raclette makers cost approximately $100.*

Cornichon *(cor-nih-SHOHN)* is the French word for gherkin. These small pickles are crisp and tart, and found in most grocery stores. Cornichons can be served as an accompaniment with raclette, pâtés, and smoked meats.

2 pounds raclette cheese with rind, preferably French

Accompaniments
1¹/₂ pounds new red potatoes, boiled

1 pound Black Forest ham, sliced

One 8-ounce jar cornichons, drained

One 8-ounce jar tiny pickled onions, drained

Freshly grated nutmeg

Freshly ground black pepper

Kosher salt

▶ Cut the cheese so that it fits into the cheese trays and so that it melts easily, such as 4x2-inch rectangles that are ¼ inch thick.

▶ Place the sliced cheese on a serving platter along with the ham, cornichons, and onions. The boiled potatoes can be left in a casserole dish with a lid to keep them warm. Put the nutmeg, salt, and pepper in little piles on a separate dessert plate. Use a raclette maker to melt the cheese according to the manufacturer's directions.

Have your guests assemble their plates as follows:

▶ Place some potatoes on the plate, top with melted cheese and smash together.

▶ Add some ham, cornichons, and onions to the plate.

▶ Sprinkle everything wtih nutmeg, salt, and pepper.

▶ Enjoy every forkful!

SERVES 6

Triple-Chocolate Chip Cookies

This recipe is based on the classic Toll House cookie recipe, with some tasty changes your friends and family will love!

CONNIE'S NOTES: *To achieve just-baked taste, microwave cookies for 30 seconds at 50 percent power and enjoy with a glass of cold milk or an espresso.*

2¼ cups flour

2 tablespoons good-quality unsweetened cocoa powder

1 teaspoon baking soda

1 teaspoon kosher salt

2 sticks (16 tablespoons) butter, softened

¾ cup granulated sugar

¾ cup firmly packed dark brown sugar

1 teaspoon pure vanilla extract

2 eggs, at room temperature

One 12-ounce package Ghirardelli or other good-quality double chocolate chips

1 cup coarsely chopped pecans, lightly toasted

▶ Preheat the oven to 375°F. Line your cookie sheets with parchment paper.

▶ In a small bowl, sift together the flour, cocoa powder, baking soda, and salt. Set aside.

▶ In a large bowl, combine the butter, sugars, and vanilla. Cream together until the ingredients form into one large piece. Add one egg at a time, beating thoroughly after each addition. Gradually add the dry ingredients mixture, and mix until blended. Stir in the chocolate chips and nuts by hand. At this point, you can chill the dough for future use.

▶ Drop by rounded tablespoons (or whatever size you want) onto the cookie sheets. Bake for 7–9 minutes. Do not overbake! When you take them out of the oven, they will continue baking. Wait 2 minutes, and transfer the cookies to wire racks to cool. Store in resealable plastic containers to maintain freshness.

MAKES 3–4 DOZEN

CHAPTER 5

ON WINE AND BEER

While this chapter is not an end all (there are plenty of great wine books for that!), it is meant to give you an overview of wine and beer and what to pair with your made-from-scratch creations. For the first time since The Gallup Poll was conducted on this topic in 1992, wine has become more popular than beer. In fact, 39 percent of Americans prefer to drink wine, and 36 percent prefer beer. Why the change? Many experts say that wine is now more affordable, of better quality, and more available than it used to be (and maybe helped by some advertising too!).

Wine 101

The best way to learn about wine and beer is to jump right in. Browse (as my husband says) in your small neighborhood wine/beverage shop, if you have one. Subscribe to various wine and food magazines. Talk to sommeliers and browse their extensive wine offerings at your favorite restaurants. Talk to the waitstaff when you are on vacation in Napa or Sonoma, California. They know where the good vineyards are located, and they know their wine! Befriend the salespeople at your neighborhood wine store. Ask lots of questions, just like you would ask your local butcher.

You will begin to understand terms like "nose," "bouquet," "finish," and "body." Tell the wine professional what you are preparing for dinner, and let her help you match the right wine to the food. If the wine is a gift, ask your hosts what the menu is so you can pair the wine appropriately. If you don't know the menu or the hosts very well, you can never go wrong with a bottle of champagne. What kind of spices and sauces are going in and on the food? These will make a huge difference regarding wine pairing. However, there are some wines that you buy and drink for the sheer pleasure, with no strings attached. Moscato d'Asti, a sparkling wine, fits into this category.

Don't forget to tell the wine professional your budget. Perry Fotopoulos, owner of Randolph Wine Cellars in Chicago, says that they stock 100 great wines under $10, so outstanding wines do not have to be expensive! Many wine stores have monthly wine tastings or wine clubs, which are excellent opportunities to taste lots of different wines from all over the world. By checking on the Internet, you should be able to find wine classes in your area, or online classes. Take a friend to the classes and explore the ever-changing world of wine. Anyone that knows a lot about wine loves to share his knowledge, so take advantage of it. You will find there are many more wines than just Merlots and Chardonnays.

Some Basics, Not "Rules" About Wine (Because There Are No Rules)

Drink what you like, but be open to trying new kinds of wine. Remember that French Chablis tastes quite different than the California version of Chablis out of a jug. French Chablis is a wonderful wine with mineral tasting qualities from the Chardonnay grape in the Burgundy region of France. The California version is something we drank very cheaply in college. Chardonnays vary with their oakiness.

Generally, red wine goes with meat, and white wine goes with white, delicate fish. If you are having very simple food, pair it with a more complex wine. If you are having very complex food, pair it with a simple wine. However, wine doesn't go with everything. Therefore think about beer with Mexican, Thai, and Indian food. Sometimes Rieslings work well with Asian food. Even champagne can work with Asian food. There are two common foods that are difficult to pair with wine: asparagus and green salads. If you add cheese, bacon, or eggs to a salad, you can easily pair it with a white wine. Otherwise, you may want to skip wine during the salad course.

Ideally, most wines should be stored at 55°F, reds should be slightly chilled, and whites should be chilled for several hours. Generally, whites are too chilled and reds are not chilled enough. If you chill a red wine for about 30–45 minutes before you plan to serve it, the temperature should be just right. A cooler red wine will have more flavor and pair better with your main dish. Also, don't forget about letting a red wine breathe a little before you drink it.

Be careful about transporting wine on airplanes in the heat of the summer. Extreme temperature changes can have a detrimental effect on wine. Keep that in mind if you pick up cases of wine in small vineyards around the United States, and travel home with it. Ideally, wine should be stored in a cool dark space and the bottles should be laid on their sides. It also helps to keep the humidity level constant in your storage area. Otherwise, the corks could crack and allow unwanted oxygen into your treasured wine.

Wine Pronunciations

Don't be intimidated by wine pronunciations. Perhaps Merlot and Chardonnay became so popular because they were too easy for all of us to pronounce.

Chardonnay (shar-dough-nay)
Sauvignon Blanc (sew-vee-nyawn-blahnc)
Riesling (rees-ling)
Gewürztraminer (guh-vertz-tra-mee-ner)
Semillon (sem-me-yawn)
Viognier (vee-oh-nyay)

Cabernet Sauvignon (cab-air-nay sew-vee-nyawn)
Merlot (mair-low)
Pinot Noir (pea-know nwahr)
Zinfandel (zin-fan-del)
Cabernet Franc (cab-air-nay frahnc)
Syrah (sir-rah)

Champagne and Sparkling Wine

The Champagne region of France is about a 90-minute drive from Paris. Only sparkling wines from this Champagne region can legally be called Champagne. All other sparkling wines in the world are sparkling wines, not Champagne. There are some excellent and inexpensive sparkling wines from Spain, Italy, and California. Oftentimes, Champagne and sparkling wine are associated with a celebration.

Some Common Toasts Around the World

American	To your health, cheers (or a personalized toast)
Bulgarian and Polish	Nazdrave *(Naz DRA-vay)*: to your health
Cantonese	Yum seng: drink and celebrate
Croatian	Zivjeli *(jeevaylee)*: cheers
Dutch	Proost: to your health
English	Cheers
French	A votre santé: health
German	Prost or Zum Wohl: cheers
Greek	Yiamas or Giamas *(Yaw-muss)*: to your health
Irish	Sláinte *(sloynta or slaan-cheh)*: to your health
Italian	Cin cin or Salute, Cent'anni: health, 100 years of life, or Alla nostra: to us or to our health
Japanese	Kampei: cheers
Korean	Kun-bae *(kunbay)*: to drink to your health
Lebanese	Soha: health
Russian	Vashe zdorovye: your health
Scandinavian	Skål *(scoal)*: Cheers
Spanish	Salud: to your health
Thai	Chai Yo: good luck
Yiddish	L'Chaim *(layhyem)*: to life or Mazel Tov: good luck

Wine Accessories

The most important wine accessories are: a corkscrew that works well for you and fits your hand, and a vacuum device and plastic stoppers. The vacuum device and plastic stoppers keep the oxygen out of red and white wine when you don't finish it. They help to preserve the flavor and aroma of the wine. These useful and inexpensive devices can be purchased at a home decorating or kitchen supply store. Of course, you probably want two types of wineglasses, larger glasses for reds and smaller ones for whites. Other accessories for down the road include: wine buckets, wine chillers, different types of quality glassware for different wines, coolers, etc. Finally, you might want to develop a system for keeping track of the wines you like. That might be as simple as a little black spiral wine book, or a sophisticated software program to record the name of the wine, vintage, purchase date and price, and your personal notes.

OTBN

OTBN stands for Open That Bottle Night. *The Wall Street Journal* invented OTBN in 2000 so that we would open that bottle of wine that we have been saving for years. Open That Bottle Night is always on the last Saturday of February. Get together with a group of friends, make a special meal, and open the bottles of wine that you are saving for something.

On Wine and Women

Here are some interesting tidbits from recent studies. Did you know that women make the majority of wine purchases in this country? Wine quality is important to women but so are the design of the label and the philosophy of the vineyard. Women are less influenced by the ratings than men. As you might expect, women tend to drink more white and rosé and men drink more red wine. Women tend to have a more developed olfactory sense than men.

To Your Health

Some health benefits of wine include: improved cognitive benefit and reduced further decline, and improved blood flow, which can help us to live longer, healthier lives.

My parting words on wine are "Drink more Riesling!" It's what most of the wine experts suggest. Greg Anderson, a self-taught wine aficionado, sums it all up, "Have fun, and enjoy the ride!"

Beer

We don't want to forget about beer. For centuries, beer and food went together in the homes of the rich and the poor in those grain-producing nations. According to beer lovers, beer can bring out the rich flavors of food as well as the grape. Just remember that beer is more filling than wine. Experiment with some of the interesting regional beers in your area. As Jim Koch, founder of Boston Beer Company said, "I've been to those wine tastings, and they actually spit it out! We beer people actually enjoy drinking." Beer pairs quite well with food too. What if you are making burgers on the grill or having pizza? Consider your old standby—beer. Beer and sausages taste great together. Don't forget that triple bock beers will taste great with a dense chocolate dessert.

CHAPTER 6

WHEN YOU GO OUT TO DINNER

So you have decided that you want to go out and have a fabulous meal. Maybe you want to have one of those dinners that you could never create at home because you don't have the necessary skills to make four different sauces, or the patience to make a quenelle. Or you just don't have the time or help to make a tedious meal. Perhaps you can't find all the exotic or fine-quality ingredients, or don't have a pan to make the tarte tatin. Maybe the most important reason of all is that you want to be waited on hand and foot, with a glass of bubbly Champagne to start, and have a decadent hook to stow your evening bag on when you arrive. Or maybe it is nothing more than you want to be able to have an adult conversation with your husband or friend without little ones underfoot at your local pizzeria! In other words—you want QUIET, and that's why you are going out to dinner without the kids. Here are some tips for dining out.

How Do You Go About Choosing a Special Restaurant?

Some of us rely on local newspaper reviews, James Beard Awards, long-term reputation, or recommendations of friends, your spouse, or companion. Some of us just have particular favorites because we know the waitstaff. Perhaps the restaurant makes an entrée or dessert that we crave. Maybe the wine list is superb, or the restaurant has been consistently outstanding time after time. For others, we just feel comfortable in the restaurant—the ambience is charming, we can go casual, and we feel like we belong. Lastly, your budget may determine whether the restaurant is a fit this month or down the road.

For your information, many professional waiters recommend avoiding their favorite restaurants on holidays, and advise dining during the week, not the weekend. They also recommend that "new" is not always better in the restaurant world. Most industry professionals go out on Sunday nights and prefer the local standby restaurants!

When Deciding on a Dining Choice, Call Ahead for a Reservation and Ask for the Dress Code

For some fine restaurants in large cities, that may take at least a month. Sometimes the concierge of your hotel can snag a hard-to-get reservation. Most fine-dining restaurants will call to confirm your reservation time, date, and size of your party a couple of days in advance. (Often in France, reservations are such a part of the culture that they are required even if you stand outside and make the reservation on your cell phone 15 minutes before!) Sometimes you may need to fill out your profile for a favorite and very popular restaurant. They will keep it in their computer database, and you may become a regular. Sometimes "regulars" can snag a last-minute reservation. Also, try one of the popular websites, opentable.com or other credit card programs to make reservations for restaurants in major cities.

If you have a special place you would like to sit in your favorite restaurant, ask for it in advance. All they can say is no. If you need a quiet section of the restaurant for a more intimate business conversation, request it. Also, let the maître d' know who will be paying for the business dinner. It saves a lot of confusion at the end of a meal and ends the dinner smoothly.

If you need to cancel the reservation, please do so out of courtesy to the restaurant business. Your no-show table could mean lost revenue of several hundred dollars or more. With computerized reservation systems, you can end up on a "black list" if you don't cancel your reservation promptly. Restaurants hate no-shows! Some restaurants take a down payments on a credit card if your party is six or more. If you are not seated within 30 minutes of your reservation, by all means discuss this with the maître d' or hostess. The fine-dining restaurants will anticipate this minor glitch and should offer you a complimentary glass of Champagne or a cocktail.

Lastly, many fine-dining restaurants do not allow cell phones in the dining room, so that everyone can have a pleasant dining experience. You may want to inquire about their cell phone policy before you make a reservation.

If you have special dietary needs or have a particular waiter that you know quite well, by all means tell this to the reservation booker, or call the maître d' directly. You will still find a maître d' in some French restaurants. A **maître d'** is simply a French term for headwaiter or house steward of a restaurant. He is the gatekeeper of the "front of the house" staff, and sets the tone for your evening. If you have theatre or symphony tickets after the meal, inform the maître d' or manager before your reservation, and when you arrive at the restaurant.

How to Be a Good Customer

Restaurants want you to be a very happy repeat customer or a "regular." They can accommodate you if they know this important information in advance. However, remember that restaurants can meet only so many special requests. The waiter will inform you if the substituted item may be priced differently, take longer to prepare, or may change the integrity of the dish. Also, steer clear of asking for your meal "on the side." You don't want to be known as an "on-the-sider!" Finally, if you have been given a

phenomenal bottle of wine and you want to take it to the restaurant, check with the maître d' first. They will probably accommodate you with a nominal corkage fee.

Professional waiters have a passion for the restaurant business and make a great living or they would be doing something else. Waiters love the "regulars" and building relationships with their customers. They relish knowing your special cocktail or just the way you like your steak. However, waiters are always being squeezed by three immutable forces: the customer, the kitchen, and the management. A good restaurant staff knows that it is not only the food of the restaurant that makes you want to return, it is also the personnel and the ambience. Maybe you like the way your linen napkin is refolded while you are in the ladies' or men's room, or the way an umbrella is waiting for you when you step out of your car or cab. They are professionals and like being given the same respect you bestow upon your family physician, dentist, or accountant. They are going to have a mutual relationship with you for several hours, and want to make it the best possible one for everyone involved.

Professional waiters know that you want to be pampered because you are taking a break from work and the kids. They feel like they are hosting a party every night. Waiters suggest politeness because they control the outcome of your evening. They recognize a phony or big shot early on. Don't pretend to know what you don't know. Waiters hate attitudes too! By all means, ask a lot of questions. They want to guide you toward the best possible dining experience, and keep you from noticing any problems in the immediate background (just like a play that goes awry and you don't realize it!). Of course, trust is an enormous part of the relationship. They have done their homework on knowing and understanding the menu and the exquisite ingredients the chef is using. Ideal customers for waiters are: ones who are enjoying themselves, trust them, and actively invest in their evening out.

Waiters are like therapists, best friends, confidantes, and sounding boards. They also learn interesting tidbits about the restaurant business, like using pickle juice to clean grills! Diners also ask for the darndest things. Somehow they think that waiters can produce duct tape, dates, Cubs baseball team flags, and even avocadoes for their meal at home tomorrow. Hubert Schwermer, Maître d'Hotel, from the 3-star Guy Savoy Restaurant in Paris, said "One of my customers asked me what was my favorite dessert?" I replied, "The black forest cake at Euro Disney!" The diner promptly pulled out his business card saying that he was the President and General Manager of Disney World Resorts!

What About Wine?

Most people are very intimidated about wine, but they shouldn't be. Many restaurant professionals are very knowledgeable about wine, as it is a very important part of the dining experience. They are trained weekly on new wines and the proper pairing of wine and food. By all means, drink what you like, but be open to your server's suggestions, or the suggestions of the **sommelier** (saw-muh-lyay). Please don't say "I just drink red or white!" Also, wine experts would probably recommend cocktails **before** the meal, not during the meal, as cocktails don't pair well with food.

Sommelier is the French term for the highly trained wine steward who is in charge of wine. They will put you at ease. Often, sommeliers can contribute as much to the enjoyment of a meal as the chefs because they help take the intimidation factor out of wine. Do not be afraid to mention your wine budget. If you feel uncomfortable ordering a lower priced bottle of wine in a corporate setting, call the sommelier in advance and tell him your wine budget. Wine can play a large part in a restaurant bill. Sommeliers will be able to find you the perfect bottle of wine in your price range. As Gary Boswell, former sommelier at Pigall's Restaurant in Cincinnati, says "We want to put you at ease to have a wonderful dining experience."

Sommeliers love sharing their extensive knowledge and passion for food and wine pairing. Sometimes restaurants have half bottles of wine for those dinners that require white for the appetizer and red for the main course. Another option is that some restaurants have 3-ounce glasses of wine or wine flights paired perfectly with each part of a tasting menu. You should also be able to order a glass of wine, port, or sherry just for a cheese course.

There are no hard and fast rules to wine selection; good food, good friends, and good cheer add a further level of enjoyment to any food and wine pairing. If you find a wine that you truly love, have the waiter write it down for you.

PHOTO © SEAN WILLIAMS

Vino Machino, Redmoon Theatre, Chicago

Generally red meat requires red wine, and white fish works best with white wine. Spicy foods are a little harder to pair with wine, so be sure and ask for advice. When you feel comfortable, branch out with some of the outstanding sweet wines with dessert courses. Also, don't be afraid to start with some of the Italian sparkling wines or Champagnes as aperitifs. In the Champagne region of France, they often drink Champagne with the entire meal!

Other Restaurant Tidbits

At fine-dining restaurants, the chef might offer you an *amuse bouche* (ah-myuz-boosh) to start your meal. This is nothing more than a French term meaning "to amuse the mouth." An *amuse bouche* is a complimentary morsel of something delicious, and a hint of more to come.

Also, if there are unusual foods on the menu like: ramps, *burratta, mignardises, spigarnello,* etc. be sure and ask the waiter to explain these ingredients, and pronounce them

for you. Part of the adventure of going out to dinner is to try exotic foods that you would not eat on an everyday basis.

Vie, a restaurant in the Chicago suburbs, explains unusual ingredients by writing definitions of these ingredients at the bottom of its menus.

How to Pay the Bill?

Generally, this is a difficult moment for all involved unless you have discussed it prior to going to the restaurant. If you have a group of four–six, you can easily split the bill evenly among two or three credit cards. Waiters are happy to accommodate you with individual credit cards. (I don't think they will take 10 individual credit cards though!) If you are a very frequent guest at the restaurant, the restaurant might set up a "house account" for you, and bill you monthly.

If it is a fun group of your best 10–15 friends, you might ask the restaurant to make up a small menu with three choices

Jean-Robert
at Pigall's,
Cincinnati, Ohio.
Jean-Robert Cavel,
owner and chef

each with an appetizer, entrée, and dessert. Tell them that you have a budget of say $50 each plus alcohol and gratuity. It is easier to have a set menu for all your friends and easier for the restaurant when there are large parties involved (see the **prix fixe** *(PREE-FIHKS)* or fixed price menu at right from De Cero restaurant in Chicago) Also, you won't have that dreaded, "I don't have enough money," or "I need a dollar back"! The end of the gathering will be just as pleasant as the beginning and the middle.

Appropriate tipping in a fine-dining restaurant is generally from 15–25 percent, depending on where you live and the tipping customs. When there is a large group involved, the restaurant may have a fixed gratuity schedule. Check on these gratuities in advance, if possible.

What to Do If You Had a Wonderful Experience
Generally a thank you, calling the waiter by name, and an appropriate tip will suffice. If the waitstaff did truly make your evening special, a $20 bill for the front of the house goes a long way! Remember their names and they will remember yours. Sometimes personal notes to the staff are much appreciated too. Remember how you felt the last time you received an unexpected thank you for a service? And if you had a less than stellar visit, let your maître d' know in a tasteful manner. Again, he wants you to be a regular. He knows that you have hundreds of choices, but you chose his restaurant. Finally, remember that in most European restaurants the customer has to request the bill. Otherwise, you might sit there long after you wanted to. On the contrary, you may receive your check before you are finished with your meal in the United States. Economics are in play here!

PRIX FIXE MENU
Corporate Party
November 16

appetizers

house salsas mild verde or spicy picante
with house-made chips

guacamole avocado, garlic, onion,
tomato, lime, cilantro, jalapeño

taco platters

ahi tuna, grilled medium rare
with mango and habanero salsa

avocado, with white onion,
roasted garlic, and crema

beef tenderloin tips, braised with
mushrooms, tomatoes, and cilantro

chipotle chicken, with mashed
pinto beans and crema

entrée choices

enchiladas, three cheese with red or
green salsa; black beans and rice

fajitas, choice of steak chicken or shrimp;
served with warm tortillas

chipotle chicken burrito, bacon mashed pinto
beans, queso, lettuce and crema

carne asada, served with bacon mashed pinto
beans, basmati rice and tortillas

dessert choices

white chocolate chip brownie with
chocolate chip ice cream

trio of sorbet

RECOMMENDED READING

La Varenne Pratique: The Complete Illustrated Cooking Course by Anne Willan.
Techniques, ingredients, and tools of classic modern cuisine with more than
2,500 full-color photographs.

*The New Food Lover's Companion: Comprehensive Definitions of Nearly 6000 Food,
Drink, and Culinary Terms* by Sharon Tyler Herbst.
Includes metric conversion formulas and metric equivalents.

The River Café Wine Primer by Joseph Delissio
Covers how to taste and evaluate wine, the wine cellar/buying wine, the vineyard and the
vintage, and the wine regions.

The Oxford Companion to Wine by Jancis Robinson.

Any Julia Child cookbook.
They may be out of print, but they can be found at book fairs and flea markets.

INDEX

Note: **Boldfaced** page references indicate recipe photographs.